The Executive Coaching Bible

The Fast and Simple Way to Elevate Your
Business Leadership and Master Effective
Communication in Just 20 Minutes a Day

Victor Greyson

Table of Contents

Introduction

Leadership is an intimidating thing. It's full of dangerous beasts that might devour you at any time. On that unsteady path, one slip, and you'll pass away from falling. There's a baddie behind every corner, ready to pounce and scare the living daylights out of you. Take the scariest story you've ever read or watched and double it by 10; that's how terrifying leadership can be.

Being a leader is the hardest position I've ever had, but I **embraced** it. I want to instill fear in those who are thinking about a career in leadership. Why? To make sure you know what you're getting into before you sign up. I hope you accept the weight of leadership and learn to value it for what it is.

Leadership is tough because it involves accepting your limitations, dealing with uncertainty, and being responsible for the well-being and success of others. For someone to become a good leader—one who welcomes challenges, learns from setbacks, and walks the path with confidence and conviction—they must first admit this fear.

We often feel both awe and fear when we hear the word "leadership" in the context of our employment. As leaders, we must also sail our own ships through unfamiliar waters, weathering storms of uncertainty and navigating the complex channels of our own personal and professional development. It's a huge deal, fraught with difficult obstacles and palpable terror. But here you are, looking for answers, motivated by a need to not merely survive but excel in your leadership role. Don't worry—you're not alone.

Breaking the Chains: Identifying Your Catalyst for Change

Let's get down to brass tacks here. You're probably here because you've hit a professional wall and realized how disheartening it is to realize you're not living up to your full potential or the standards of people around you. Being stuck in a rut, wanting change but not knowing how to make it, is a painful position to be in.

Maybe you're about to step into a new position that will require you to have stronger leadership and communication abilities, and the pressure to do so is mounting. Perhaps you already have the communication skills necessary to be a successful corporate leader, but you feel you might have a greater influence, achieve greater success, and forge stronger bonds with your team.

What makes this book unique? What sparked your drive to become a better leader? Each reader has their own individual catalyst, a guiding light that has brought them here. Whether it's a sense of unfulfillment in your current situation or a never ending desire for advancement that led you here, you've recognized a need and are actively seeking a solution.

What's In It For You?

Now, let's talk about the benefits or what you may expect to get out of your journey through these pages. This book is more than a manual; it's a fast track to positive change. You will become very self-aware and get to know your core leadership values, as well as your strengths and flaws. These are important skills for both personal and professional growth. These changes will not only make your leadership skills better, but they will take them to whole new levels. Your capacity for effective communication will develop into a power that can be used to bring people together and promote mutual appreciation.

As you navigate the chapters, you'll discover yourself growing more adaptive in the face of changes and obstacles. Insurmountable obstacles will become steppingstones. Moving up the corporate ladder will no longer be a pipe dream but a real possibility. Your personal and professional networks will grow, and your impact will spread like waves across the water. The goal here isn't simply professional advancement; it's also the pinnacle of your own happiness, contentment, and success.

The A.C.E. Leadership Progression Framework: A Roadmap to Success

Step up your game as a leader using the A.C.E. Leadership Progression Framework, which emphasizes Acquiring Foundational Leadership Knowledge, Cultivating and Advancing Leadership Skills, and Excelling in Leadership. It's more than simply a set of directions; it's a carefully plotted course that will get you where you need to go swiftly and effortlessly. This framework sets us apart—it's structured, actionable, and time-efficient, designed for concrete outcomes in both your career and personal life.

Here's the big question: How is this different from other solutions you've tried or that competitors are offering? The key is in the uniqueness of our approach. This isn't a cookie-cutter guide to improving your life; it's a personalized plan for becoming an effective leader. It's not just empty words; it's a promise to arm you with the knowledge and resources you need to make a difference. It won't take up too much of your time but will be well worth your while in the long run.

Perhaps you're asking, "Does this actually work?" The radical success of our method has been attested to by numerous clients, some of whom are well known in their fields. Think about how your life will change when you learn the secrets that A-listers have used to become more effective leaders.

Envision yourself in the future, having made important contributions to the company and rising through the ranks to senior positions, feeling completely fulfilled in your work, and receiving widespread acclaim for your achievements. It's not some far-off mirage, but rather the final destination.

Why Trust the Author?

I've been where you are now, so I can help you along the way. Challenges are familiar to me because I've been through them. My insights aren't just theories; they come from my own experiences in the real world. The path was more challenging, the checkpoints fewer and far between, and the feeling of accomplishment more elusive before I had this information. By writing this book, I hope to lend a helping hand and impart some wisdom gained from the front lines of leadership.

In the pages that follow, you'll uncover the 'new' information that can transform your approach to leadership. That knowledge would have made my journey easier and more rewarding if I had had it earlier. This is the ideal book for you; it's a guide written with compassion, strategic planning, and a sincere desire to see you succeed.

As you go out on this adventure, keep in mind that leadership is about more than just reaching the top; it's about inspiring and empowering those around you to join you. Join me as I help you reach new heights by realizing your full potential. Welcome to Leadership Unleashed: A Journey to Excellence!

Part 1:

Acquiring Foundational Leadership

Knowledge

Chapter 1:

Leadership Alchemy: Crafting the Cornerstones for Success

Before you become a leader, success is all about growing yourself. After you become a leader, success is about growing others. —Jack Welch

Let's be honest: This isn't the kind of leadership advice you normally hear. You won't be thrown into jargon or forced to repeat leadership lines over and over again. We're going to get down and dirty to help you make your own leadership personality.

This isn't your typical motivational section. This is the beginning of your leadership journey, and you need to set the framework now. It's like laying the cornerstone for a brand-new skyscraper. This isn't the place to skimp, would it?

In the next pages, we won't merely be discussing leadership theories in general terms. Here we get down to the real business; namely, exploring your greatest assets, your greatest weaknesses, and the ideals that speak to you in your quietest moments.

Finding Your True Leadership Self

Being a great leader isn't only about showing off your talents; it's also about showing resilience in the face of adversity and remaining steadfast in times of calm as well as chaos. How you care for your team's mental and emotional health is an integral part of the mosaic that makes up your leadership reputation.

Every contact in the world of leadership reveals something about who you are and how willing you are to take on difficulties and embrace opportunities. If you want to get to the heart of who you are as a leader, you need to take an honest look at your own perspective and the way you go about your business each day.

Now, let's dissect what makes a leader, without resorting to clichés and in a way that speaks to your personal leadership journey:

Behavior

As a leader, your choices aren't predetermined; they're an expression of the values you hold dear. How you choose to live your life is what defines you. Pay close attention to how you talk to your team for a moment. Are you creating a place where people feel safe enough to be themselves?

Interpersonal Skills

A psychologically secure environment can be created for your team by cultivating trustworthy relationships, which requires strong interpersonal skills. Think about your social skills, identify areas in which you could grow, and work to strengthen the relationships you currently have.

Mentality

The way you feel about your team affects the way you act. Leaders who prioritize compassion and empathy take a different path than those who don't. In your pursuit of leadership, let your attitude serve as a guide.

Values

Your values are the north star by which you navigate your daily life. Explore your core values, the areas where you simply won't budge, and the factors that are most important to you while working with others.

Beliefs And Presumptions

You need to dig deep into your subconscious to unearth your hidden prejudices, assumptions, and beliefs. The most important thing is to recognize and understand them. Do you believe certain things even if you don't have proof? How do you avoid letting your personal convictions get in the way of working with your team?

Building and Keeping a Positive Leadership Identity

Now that you know what makes you tick as a leader, you can start making changes that will have a lasting impact on your team. Let's get into specific advice for your leadership path.

Stick with Your Values

Leaders are not made by titles but by their actions. It is essential for leaders of any experience level to have a firm connection to their own values. All that you do should reflect these values and help your team work toward its objectives.

Embrace the Growth Mindset

No successful leader ever believed they were invincible. Responsibility and the ability to grow from setbacks are the cornerstones of greatness. Recognize your human fallibility, encourage a growth mentality, and dedicate yourself to ongoing improvement. Your team's impression of you will be shaped in a significant way by how open and honest you are with them.

Consider Problems to Be Opportunities

Rather than being sources of anxiety, leaders should view difficulties as opportunities. In doing so, they shed light on potential roadblocks. In a world as dynamic as ours, challenges are to be expected. Consider them opportunities to learn about previously unknown approaches. Involve your group and reliable friends; their insights may reveal opportunities you had missed. This approach suggests that you are a leader who places a premium on exploration and originality.

Accept the Challenges Before You

A strong sense of leadership identity promotes a psychologically secure workplace. Realize that everything you say and do with your team matters. Having a positive sense of who you are as a leader encourages positive interactions, which can help you overcome any challenges that may emerge. Leadership, keep in mind, is not just about being in charge; it is also about being a positive influence on those you lead.

Building Blocks of Effective Leadership

Leadership isn't something you get at; rather, it's a continuing process of development and change. Leadership is about more than simply keeping the ship on course; it's also about rallying the troops to do something. In that case, how does a person achieve such a level of mastery and authority in their chosen field? Here's my take.

Integrity

Being an effective leader starts with always doing the right thing. It's about creating an environment where everyone feels welcome and valued, regardless of their position. Leadership should inspire, so that those who take part come away from it feeling better for having done so. When persons in positions of authority misuse their power, hoard their benefits, engage in dishonesty, or violate the group's ideals, the integrity of the organization suffers. A leader who is worth following is reliable, impartial, and answerable.

Accountability

At its core, being a leader means taking responsibility for not only your own acts but also those of the people you are in charge of. Real leaders not only expect but also instill accountability in their subordinates. They foster a sense of community responsibility that encourages people to take action and see a problem through to its conclusion. The best leaders stop their followers from neglecting their responsibilities and help them face the inevitable difficulties of starting anything new.

Learning

Leadership goes beyond hierarchical systems of authority. Instead of relying on the knowledge of a select few leaders, it uses the brainpower of the whole group. An in-depth familiarity with the problem and its potential resolutions is essential for arriving at the best choices. Inspiring others to think critically about problems and develop novel approaches is a hallmark of strong leadership. The goal is to create a culture where learning is not only encouraged but also valued as a way of life.

Promoting Mutual Learning

Leadership must encourage free-flowing dialogue and set up a system for sharing knowledge and ideas in order to foster a culture of learning. In addition to providing a safe environment and outlining expectations, leaders can encourage productive teamwork by simply listening to their teammates. When problems develop, leaders should keep the spotlight off of themselves and on the problem at hand.

Leaders, in their efforts to foster civility and teamwork, should moderate discussions so that no one person—including the leader—takes control. To show their humility, they should respond positively to questions and criticism, encouraging participation from everybody. It is vital to enable problems and insights to arise before rushing to a solution that could suppress key contributions.

Embracing Authenticity

Being authentic means keeping true to your values, goals, and self as a leader. Trust and loyalty are gained by leaders who are authentic and consistent. They are confident in their own abilities and shortcomings and lead with integrity since they don't try to be someone they're not. Keep in mind that people follow genuine leaders, not those who try to be flawless.

Cultivating Empathy

To be a good leader, you need to be able to put yourself in the shoes of those you're leading. Going through their feelings and seeing things from their point of view is what it's all about. Which brings us to empathy. Being emotionally intelligent helps people form stronger bonds with one another, which in turn creates a more welcoming and accepting community. It helps leaders understand what their team members need and make choices that put the health and happiness of everyone first.

Promoting Collaboration

To lead is not to perform an act of heroism from on high, but rather to rally others around a common cause. In a team with a strong culture of collaboration, everyone's opinion matters. It promotes a wide range of opinions and approaches, with the understanding that the best results come from working together.

Being a Role Model

What we do speaks louder than what we say. Your team will follow the example you set as the leader. Be there, do the work, and model the attitudes and actions you want to see from your team. When leaders set the bar high, others are motivated to follow suit, fostering an environment where everyone strives to do their best.

Promoting Respect

Respect is a two-way street, not a one-way alley, just like trust and honesty. Everyone in the team, regardless of rank, is entitled to and merits to be treated with the utmost respect. Respect decreases tension, promotes fairness, stops harassment, and eventually increases employee involvement in their work. When workers believe they are valued, they are more motivated to work together, which is good for the team's productivity. Being respectful shows through your honesty, kindness, fair punishment, and open communication, which are all important parts of being a good leader.

Fostering Empathy

Have you ever been in a scenario where you wanted your sentiments to be acknowledged but they were instead ignored? Such a situation is all too common and can make a person feel unappreciated and misunderstood. When leaders show empathy and care for their team members, they elevate them from faceless machines to indispensable coworkers. Compassion fosters a culture of caring reciprocity among people of all backgrounds and experiences. When employees believe that their contributions matter, they are more likely to go above and beyond. Take the time to get to know your team members, offer direction, and be sensitive to their needs to show that you truly care.

Embracing Self-Awareness

Self-awareness is at the center of any successful leadership structure. The foundation of all values is courage, and the engine of any leadership system is self-awareness. Leaders under your wing need to know they can count on you no matter what comes their way, and you should be there to help them figure out how to handle difficult situations. Self-aware leaders will do the following:

- Hold their values

- Find the sweet spot between internal and external motivators

- Put together a terrific supporting team

- Live a full and balanced life

Designing a Growth Mindset

A growth mindset is not just an idea; it's a way of thinking that says you can get better at anything by working hard, taking calculated risks, and listening to and learning from the advice of those more experienced than yourself.

12

Professor Carol Dweck of the University of Stanford in the United States coined the phrase "growth mindset" in her 2006 book *Mindset: The New Psychology of Success*, which explores the profound impact of an individual's underlying attitude about their intelligence and learning potential on their performance (Boksic, 2023).

According to Professor Dweck's findings, there is a significant difference between individuals who believe their capabilities are fixed at birth and those who believe they may improve upon them. People who have a growth mentality see setbacks as chances for personal development and prefer to take risks and expand their knowledge base rather than play it safe. With this new outlook, leaders can create an environment where change is welcomed, and success is expected.

More than just a passing fad, the "growth mindset" is a significant ideology that determines how you respond to difficult situations and new information. Let's break down the essentials of developing a growth mindset in your leadership role:

Learning to Think According to a Growth Mindset

Mindsets can be fixed- or growth-oriented, and the latter is predicated on the conviction that a person's talents and IQ can be enhanced via focused effort and education. Leaders with a growth mindset view difficulties as lessons, value hard work as the key to success, and refuse to give up in the face of adversity. Having this understanding as a starting point is crucial in order to foster a growth mindset and pursue a path of constant progress.

Focus on the Process, Not Just the Outcome

The process is just as important as the end result in a growth mentality. Leaders should stop focusing so much on the final product and start appreciating the journey there. Recognize the progress that has been made, take note of what may be improved upon, and urge your team to see obstacles not as insurmountable barriers but as opportunities for growth.

Plan Ahead

One of the most important aspects of developing a growth mindset is setting and working toward goals. Leaders should set objectives that are both challenging and attainable for themselves and their teams. These objectives serve as signposts, giving one a feeling of purpose and direction. Create a plan of action that is in line with the growth mindset and helps you achieve your long-term goals.

Use an Efficient Method of Leadership

Leaders who have a growth mindset are more likely to use strategies that foster personal progress and professional mastery. Adopt a coaching mindset, act as a mentor, and foster a culture where innovation and risk-taking are rewarded. Align your leadership approach with growth concepts, with an emphasis on teamwork and ongoing education.

Seek Feedback

Growth can't happen without feedback. Leaders should always be on the lookout for opinions and suggestions from those around them. Constructive criticism reveals weak spots and directs one's growth as a learner. Foster an environment where people care about one other and are willing to provide and receive constructive criticism.

Get Ideas from Others

Knowledge sharing is essential for a growth attitude. Leaders should make an effort to learn from others around them, both inside and outside of the team. Participate in workshops and look for mentors who can help you out. Your own leadership development will benefit from hearing about other people's experiences, and the team's growth mentality will be strengthened as a whole.

Including these practices in your leadership style can help you develop a growth mindset and inspire your team to embrace change and progress together. The end result? A flexible and innovative approach to leadership that drives both individual and collective success.

Figuring Out Your Weaknesses and Strengths

To fully grasp your leadership potential, you must take stock of your many strengths and admit the places where you may use improvement. Here's a comprehensive look at how to identify and evaluate your own areas of strength and improvement:

Feedback from Teammates, Mentors, and Coworkers:

Actively involve your team, mentors, and coworkers to get different points of view on how you lead. Foster an environment where honest feedback is given and received by promoting open and honest communication. Together, you can learn a lot about your strengths and places that might need more work by working together.

Common Leadership Strengths

- Powerful leaders are excellent communicators who can persuade and inspire their followers. They pay close attention so that their words are not only heard but also grasped by the receiver. A well-communicated team is a well-informed and cohesive team.

- Effective leaders are known for their ability to see the value in others and delegate tasks accordingly. Individuals benefit from more autonomy, skill development, and leadership time spent on more strategic endeavors when authority is delegated.

- Leaders who take the initiative to make things happen for their teams and organizations are the ones who ultimately get the benefits. They are always looking for ways to improve and are constantly pushing others around them to do the same. The initiative encourages an energetic and forward-thinking leadership approach.

- Great leaders are dedicated to always getting better. They have a growth attitude and foster an environment where everyone is constantly improving and striving for more.

Common Leadership Weaknesses

- Leaders who place an excessive amount of value on being liked may avoid making difficult choices or giving constructive criticism, despite the fact that both are vital to effective leadership. It's important to find a mix between being friendly and being a strong leader.

- A failure to comprehend and control your own emotions, as well as those of others, is a key component of emotional intelligence. Leaders who are emotionally numb may have trouble fostering teamwork, showing empathy, and resolving conflicts.

- Constantly placing the blame on others is a surefire way to turn the workplace into a hostile place to work. A key component of good leadership is taking responsibility and putting effort into finding solutions rather than assigning blame.

Improving Your Leadership Capabilities

When you know where you stand in terms of your leadership abilities, you can work to improve them in a methodical and purposeful way. Listed below is a complete manual for honing your leadership skills through deliberate practice:

Leverage Your Strengths

If you want to succeed as a leader, you need to first figure out what those strengths are. When it comes to directing and inspiring your team, play to your strengths by capitalizing on the advantages your strengths provide.

Clear Communication

Strong leaders understand the importance of good communication. Develop your ability to convey ideas clearly and effectively with the intention of fostering productive team interactions.

Become a Better Listener:

Take an interest in the thoughts, ideas, and criticisms of your coworkers. Engage in compassionate listening to better comprehend others' points of view and forge meaningful bonds with them.

Modify How You Talk to People:

Recognize and accommodate the varying communication styles of your team members. This helps everyone on the team understand each other and work together better.

Optimize Delegation

Strategic task delegation is a cornerstone of competent leadership. Figure out what each team member is good at and give them jobs that fit those strengths. This not only gives your team more agency, but also frees you up to concentrate on more important tasks.

Initiative Expansion

Motivate your staff to adopt a proactive attitude. The best way to get individuals to step up and own their responsibilities and make meaningful contributions to the success of your organization is to praise and reward them when they demonstrate initiative.

Developing a Hunger for Excellence

Set an example of constant growth and improvement. Show that you have a growth mentality by actively seeking to improve your skills and knowledge. The rest of the group will likely follow suit if this is the example set.

Exploring Leadership Assessment Tools

Given the many choices, it can be hard to find your way around the many leadership testing tools that are out there. That's why I've put together this list of the best leadership testing tools available right now to help you find the best ones for your needs.

360 Feedback from SurveySparrow

SurveySparrow 360 Feedback is one of the best 360-degree feedback tools because it makes it easy to get detailed feedback on a leader's work. The platform has a simple user interface and blends conversational style with chat-like surveys, which ensures an amazing 40% response rate. Careful examination of the collected data reveals the manager's strengths, weaknesses, and general style of leadership.

A report-savvy screen that finds trends adds to the proof of its usefulness. Starting at $59 each assessment, the Basic plan is SurveySparrow's most affordable option, while the Advanced plan gives users access to a wider range of scales and the Forever Free plan is available indefinitely but with fewer features. There is a free sample for people who want to try out the tool for themselves.

Myers-Briggs Type Indicator (MBTI)

The Myers-Briggs Type Indicator (MBTI) is an outstanding evaluation tool, and it has been around for more than 50 years, making it a true veteran in the area. When compared to the DISC test, the MBTI test is a little more complicated but still very useful. The test results give you a lot of information about a person's personality and skills.

The MBTI classifies people into one of 16 different types, each represented by a different four-letter acronym:

- Thinking (T) vs Feeling (F)

- Extroverted (E) vs Introverted (I)

- Sensing (S) vs Intuition (N)

- Judging (J) vs Perceiving (P)

Although the MBTI is a useful instrument, it does require that the user be well-versed in the four-letter combinations in order to draw any conclusions from the results. The price is free.

USC's Leadership Style Self-Assessment

USC's Leadership Style Self-Assessment is based on the important idea that correct self-perception is the key to reaching your full potential. The test will reveal your individual leadership style, helping you and your team work together more effectively. In order to maintain morale and foster teamwork, it is important to place an emphasis on mutual understanding. Understanding your own leadership style might help you make positive changes and progress. The six types that are being thought of are Contrarian, Front-Line, Metamodern, Postmodern, and Transformational. While it does a great job of identifying distinct styles, it provides little insight into the relative merits of different people. Despite this, you can access it for free for the rest of your life, making it a great option if you want to improve your leadership skills on a budget.

The Gallup Strengths Finder (Formerly, The Clifton StrengthsFinder)

If you want to know what your strengths are, Gallup's Strengths Finder is the tool for you. It focuses on your strengths instead of your flaws. This popular assessment reveals specifics on where you shine and how you can improve your weaker spots without sacrificing your strengths. While it's useful for one-on-one sessions, team settings are where it really falls short. However, for a one-time fee of $49.99, the tool is a worthwhile investment for people who want to learn more about their weaknesses and how to improve.

MindTools Leadership Skills Assessment

An 18-question questionnaire called the MindTools leading Skills Assessment gives a full picture of a person's leading abilities. Examining your performance in a variety of work settings, the survey will help you determine where you excel and where you could use some leadership training. Three key character factors determine the final outcomes of this assessment:

- Self-Confidence

- Outlook and attitude of the person

- Emotional Intelligence

You have the chance to take a more in-depth test after being told what kind of boss you are. Afterward, an informative piece goes into great detail about the particular leadership trait that was found. With free access, the MindTools Leadership Skills Assessment stands out. Because it is easy to reach, it is a useful tool for people who want to improve their leadership skills but don't have a lot of money.

Establishing Your Leadership Values

Your leadership approach and your subsequent choices are grounded in your core values. When setting your leadership values, here are some important things to keep in mind:

Consider Your Values

Explore your identity by learning more about the values and beliefs that shape you. Consider the events, people, and ideals in your life that have contributed to the formation of your character. To make good judgments and moves in your personal and professional life, you must first comprehend the values that serve as your compass.

Determine Your Essential Leadership Values

Find your true north when it comes to leadership values. These, as you see it, are the fundamentals of good leadership. You can choose any values that help you achieve your ideal of leadership effect, such as honesty, openness, compassion, and responsibility.

Align Personal and Core Leadership Values

Make sure your core values as a leader align with your own personal values. Consider how your personal beliefs fit with the values needed for a leadership position. By coming into alignment in this way, a genuine basis for authentic leadership is created.

Ask for Feedback

Actively seek out feedback from teammates, mentors, and peers from different angles. Think about how people will interpret your leadership based on your values. This outside information is extremely helpful in fostering both self-awareness and personal development.

Put Your Shared Values Into Practice

Turn the values you've found into actions you can take. Exhibit these values in your method of leadership on a regular basis Whether it's encouraging open conversation, upholding moral standards, or encouraging people to work together, show your values in the way you lead every day.

Keep Reflecting and Refining

Respect the ever-changing nature of leadership values. Keep tabs on how well they perform in practical situations. As you take on new challenges and learn from new experiences, be willing to grow and refine. Your values as a leader will always be effective if you take this flexible approach.

Chapter 2:

Developing the Leader's Mindset

The mind is everything. What you think, you become. —Buddha

This saying really hits home when it comes to being a good leader. In this eye-opening chapter, we delve deep into the minds of visionary leaders and discover what sets them apart. The key to realizing your full potential as a leader is right here. This is more than a theoretical study; it's a how-to manual for developing the mental attitude that will catapult you to the top ranks of leadership. The journey through these pages will reveal your thoughts' enormous influence on your leadership development.

Because leadership is always changing, this exploration is even more important than before. An old way of thinking won't help you succeed in today's dynamic world, but a fresh perspective will. This chapter isn't just a bunch of ideas; it's a set of tools to help you reform your mental habits.

You must be willing to question long-held beliefs, welcome uncertainty, and change the way you approach problems radically. The wisdom contained within is more than just words; it is the cornerstone upon which a future-oriented leadership structure can be built. The mind is more than a means of transportation as you set sail; it is the control center from which you will navigate your vessel of leadership into new territory.

Accepting Challenges as a Key to Success in Leadership

Taking on new challenges is not merely a good idea, but a powerful tool for climbing the professional ladder in today's fast-paced world. The advice, "Take on challenges as opportunities for growth," goes beyond being a cliché and is very true. This part explores the ideas behind this advice and figures out how it affects career growth, skill development, and the pursuit of gaining useful experiences.

Being Open to Challenges Can Be Powerful

We all face challenges in our careers, but how we deal with them is what ultimately determines our success or failure. If we have an optimistic view of challenges, we can use it as a springboard for growth. Looking at challenging tasks and commitments not as burdens but as opportunities could completely change our outlook on them.

Building Resistance and Flexibility

There is no better way to develop the attributes of resilience and adaptability, which are essential in today's hectic work environment, than to actively seek out and accept new challenges. By stepping out of our comfort zones and taking on new tasks, we gain valuable life experiences that improve our ability to deal with uncertainties. With the right frame of mind, we can gracefully adapt to new circumstances and overcome setbacks.

Mastering the Art of Leadership

When you're working on hard projects, you often have to lead your team through uncharted waters. This training as a leader is priceless since it improves our skills at leading others and making an impact on their lives. The experience we gain from taking on difficult tasks prepares us to lead and motivate different teams to achieve their full potential.

Gaining New Skills

Problem solving is like getting an accelerated degree in professional development. In the face of adversity, we can learn something new, gain some perspective, or improve our arsenal of strategies.

Accepting the Unfamiliar

When you're up for the challenge, you'll be propelled into unexplored territory, which is a breeding ground for creativity and innovation. Being forced to think outside of the box helps you develop a growth mentality that's open to new experiences and ideas. Your willingness to try new things can lead to breakthrough ideas and techniques that will help you advance in your field.

Conquering Your Fear of Failure

Professional success is often hindered by the crippling fear of failure. Addressing problems head-on can be an effective method of dealing with this kind of anxiety. Through doing things that, at first, seem impossible, you slowly gain confidence in your skills. Each win serves as proof of your abilities, allowing you to gradually overcome your fear of failure while simultaneously growing your confidence.

Establishing Explicit Goals

Clear goals are very important when you are facing problems. Determine what it is you need to do to succeed at the task at hand. Establishing concrete goals at the outset helps direct your efforts and keeps you motivated throughout the process.

Self-Care: A Priority

A lot of mental and physical work goes into getting through tough situations. Self-care must be a priority if you want to stay healthy during the process. Give your energy and attention to things that will help you feel refreshed, like working out, meditating, or spending time with the people you care about.

Searching for Advice and Mentors

Don't be afraid to ask for help when you're in a tough spot. Learn from the experiences of more knowledgeable coworkers or mentors who have dealt with issues that are similar to your own. The viewpoints and strategies they provide to get over challenges are invaluable.

The Proactive Approach

Many executives in today's fast-paced business environment are caught up in what amounts to a never-ending loop of pressing problems. Unfortunately, this reactive way of working makes it harder for managers to provide real added value through strategic strategies and quick decisions. This tendency toward reaction has become so pervasive across organizations of all sizes that it is difficult to encourage a more proactive mindset among people.

Breaking away from this engrained practice appears paradoxical, especially since trying to take a proactive strategy may feel like going swimming against the tide. But what if we've had the answer to this problem for nearly 60 years? This is true when talking about the manufacturing business.

What Exactly is Proactive Leadership?

When it comes to management, being proactive means doing more than just reacting to current problems; rather, it means remaining one step ahead of the competition by utilizing active management abilities and methods. Using this method means actively seeking to make things better all the time, whether it's in terms of output, quality of work, the safety and health of team members, or other choices that affect total performance. Benefits of proactive leadership, made possible by active supervision, include improved morale and productivity among workers and a more consistent demonstration of the company's basic values.

How to Manage Proactively?

A proactive manager use both strategy and hands-on measures to guarantee that goals are not only accomplished but surpassed. The following is a rundown of the important steps:

Strategic Points Checklist

You should start by listing the strategic milestones that have the most bearing on your responsibilities. If there are any vital checkpoints that are missing from the plan, add them in.

Validating Checkpoints

Set up a way to make sure that checkpoints are valid. Define roles and make sure everyone knows what is expected of them. Methods of validation, expected outcomes, and timetables for accomplishing goals should be detailed.

Sync Team Time

Check to see if the way your team spends their time is in line with the objectives. The key is to zero in on the time-sucking aspects of your everyday routine and get rid of them.

On-the-Spot Supervision

Practice daily "seeing for yourself" active supervision, as advocated by the Gemba Walk. By doing so, you can rest assured that your expectations and those of others will be in sync.

Reduced Stress from Extra Work

Spend a big chunk of your time (at least 30%) on determining preventative measures instead of fixing problems after they happen. Individualized training, consistent follow-ups, clear explanations of the big picture, and morale surveys all fall under this category.

Effective Time Management

Stress how carefully you need to plan your schedule. The more time you put into preparation, the more prepared you will be to weigh the benefits of waiting and taking action during times of crisis. With this method, you'll be forced to set priorities in order of significance.

Assess Proactive Management

Proactive management should be examined frequently. Take a step back and assess how close you came to your "ideal week," then figure out what went wrong and how to fix it. Taking the time to reflect improves responsiveness and productivity.

Remember that emergencies will arise, but that they shouldn't take up too much of your time if you subscribe to the idea of proactive management. It's all about finding a happy medium, while keeping your sights set squarely on your long-term goals.

Building Resilience

A key part of being a good leader is having the resilience to deal with problems and get back on your feet. Leaders who are resilient can deal with challenges, get back on track after failures, and keep going when things get tough. This trait is not only important for personal growth, but it's also important for keeping team relations positive.

High-performing leaders put a lot of effort into building resilience because they know how important it is for their careers. Professor Kohlrieser pointed out that a place where there is a lot of strife and burnout is a big problem for long-term leadership. When two high-profile executives in Switzerland killed themselves in 2013, it made the need for resilience even more clear (Kohlrieser, 2022). This shows how important it is for leaders to be strong when dealing with the challenges of the workplace.

Controlling Factors

To become more resilient, you need to take responsibility for your actions and focus on the things you can control instead of focusing on the things you can't. Break down problems into parts that you can handle. This will give you the power to deal with them in a planned way. This change in attitude strengthens personal control and lessens the effect of outside factors, which builds resilience.

Physical Toughness

Physical health is an important part of being resilient. Prioritize activities that make you physically stronger, like regular exercise, healthy eating, and getting enough rest. A healthy body makes you mentally strong, giving you the energy and stamina to face obstacles.

Plan for Increasing Resilience

The development of a strategy to boost resilience is an example of proactive planning. Find possible sources of worry and setbacks and make a list of specific things that can be done to lessen their effects. Include ways to deal with stress, people who can help you, and activities that you do for yourself in your plan. Review and improve this plan on a regular basis to keep it up to date with changing circumstances and build a strong base for long-term problems.

Get the Right Frame of Mind

Developing resilience requires adopting a growth-oriented and proactive mentality, which is something that this book talks about extensively. It means committing to always seeing problems as chances to learn and grow, keeping a positive mindset, and having an adaptable point of view. You can build a strong attitude that will help you navigate the tricky world of leadership by taking the ideas in this and the following chapters to heart.

Self-Leadership

Being resilient starts with being able to lead yourself. Taking charge of your ideas, feelings, and actions is what it means. Develop self-awareness to understand what sets you off and how you react to it. This will help you make decisions when things get tough. Self-regulation helps you stay calm when things get tough, and a growth attitude helps you keep learning. Self-leadership not only makes you more resilient, but it also sets an example for people in your circle of influence.

Team Strength

It's not just about an individual's abilities; resilience also affects how a team works together. Creating a supportive and collaborative setting is an important part of making a team more resilient. Encourage people to talk to each other, work together, and have a feeling of purpose. Offer tools for learning new skills and dealing with stress. By creating a strong team culture, you build a group strength that can handle problems together, boosting each member's ability to stay strong and do well when things go wrong.

Self-Doubt: Major Roadblock

For leaders in particular, self-doubt may be a crippling barrier to achievement and confidence. Though uncertainty and anxiety are normal human emotions, giving in to them might keep us from realizing our greatest potential. Nonetheless, there are actions we can take; the following are various methods for overcoming doubt and boosting confidence in your own leadership skills.

Recognize and Embrace Self-Doubt

The first step toward overcoming self-doubt is admitting that you have it. It's important for leaders to recognize these emotions without passing judgment because they're part of human nature. When we allow ourselves to acknowledge our self-doubt, it frees us to take preventative measures to deal with it.

Pay Attention to Your Accomplishments

Instead of focusing on your weaknesses, try thinking about your skills and the things you've done well in the past. By continuously reflecting on their accomplishments, reaffirming their confidence, and constructing a positive mentality that fights uncertainty, leaders can establish a self-affirming narrative.

Establish Reasonable Goals

The best way to overcome self-doubt is to prepare for success by setting reasonable objectives. Setting realistic goals and breaking down bigger goals into steps that are easier to reach is what leaders need to do. Feeling like you've accomplished something and having faith in your ability to handle difficulties are both boosted by this method.

Dive into Self-Compassion

Learning to be kind to yourself is a useful skill to have on hand for those times when you're having second thoughts. Those in positions of authority should be kind to themselves, accepting that struggles and failures are universal experiences. Self-compassion builds resilience, which helps leaders persevere through adversity.

Turn Your Negative Thinking Around

Changing the way they think about bad thoughts can help leaders get over self-doubt. You can actively question and restructure negative thought patterns instead of dwelling on what you see as your flaws. You can foster a more optimistic and self-reliant frame of mind by reorienting your attention to positive concepts and chances for growth.

As Always, Look for Feedback

One important way to get over self-doubt is to keep asking for feedback and help. Positive comments from coworkers and mentors can help you learn new things, and networks of people who support you can give you hope and a new point of view. By working together, leaders can reflect more clearly, increase self-assurance, and tackle difficult situations with more ease.

Nurturing a Success Vision

Great leaders stand out from the rest because they have a simple but compelling vision at the top of their minds. A leader's vision serves as a north star, influencing the course of the organization's daily operations and long-term planning. A company's success is directly tied to its leaders' ability to see the big picture, so its vision is more than just words on a plaque. A foundational part of any company is its vision, which should include its goals and core values. It needs to be motivating while still based on truth so that it can guide team members and leaders. Follow the steps below to nurture yours effectively!

Sketch Out

The first step in turning an idea into reality is conceptualization. As a compass, a team's leaders should create a compelling vision that everyone can rally around. To do this, you need to describe the future you want, set goals, and explain a common purpose that motivates everyone to work together.

Share

After a shared vision has been developed, there must be open lines of communication. For their team to fully understand and support the goal, leaders should say it strongly, consistently, and with a lot of passion. To do this, it's necessary to use a number of channels of communication to guarantee that everyone is on the same page.

Syncing Your Decisions

For leaders to effectively support a vision, they must make sure that their choices and actions are in line with the vision itself. For this to happen, leaders must make decisions that support the vision's beliefs, objectives, and main goal, which means taking a steady and honest approach to leadership.

Nurture

To nurture someone, you have to give them constant care and attention. Leaders are responsible for creating an atmosphere that allows the vision to remain current and flexible in the face of change. This may entail refining methods, addressing problems, and celebrating successes in order to maintain the vision's vitality and keep it moving forward.

Embody

Leaders, ultimately, must set an example by acting and making decisions in accordance with the vision. This genuine kind of leadership reminds everyone how important the goal is, and it creates an environment where everyone feels like they have a part in making it a reality. Leadership that communicates the vision for the future motivates participants to work together toward a common goal.

Part 2:

Cultivating and Advancing Leadership

Skills

Chapter 3:

Effective Communication 101

The most important thing in communication is hearing what isn't said. —Peter Drucker

Communication has far-reaching effects that go well beyond the words themselves; it may mold company culture, propel progress, and bring people closer together. If you want to be taken seriously as a leader, you need to master this skill.

In today's business world, the ability to communicate effectively is more than just a necessity; it's a game changer. If you don't communicate well, you will lose a lot of money, have low morale, and not meet your success goals. According to research conducted by the Economist Intelligence Unit, poor communication costs large companies an average of $64.2 million per year and puts smaller businesses at risk of losing $420,000 per year (The CEO Publication, 2023).

Still, the effects of good communication goes beyond numbers. It's the medium by which top executives motivate their teams and steer their organizations through times of transition. Read on to learn how to become a more influential leader through the transforming power of clear and persuasive communication. If you're new to the complex landscape of leadership, this chapter will serve as your guide. By the end of this chapter, you will have not only comprehended but also actively applied the transforming ideas of active listening and helpful criticism.

Understanding the Basics of Good Communication

One definition of leadership is the ability to motivate others to take action that advances shared goals. Communication is a leader's most potent weapon for accomplishing this. Trust, goal alignment, and positive change are all made possible through clear and concise communication. Lack of communication can lead to misunderstandings, which in turn can strain relationships and stand in the way of progress. If you want to be a better leader, here are eight ways to improve your communication skills.

Authenticity

Be sincere and honest. Avoid using corporate jargon or putting on a false persona; instead, just be yourself when communicating. Communicate in a way that reflects your identity, values, and experiences. Being a leader who is true to themselves inspires loyalty and admiration from their followers. Choose authenticity above flowery language. Don't wear masks; people won't follow something that doesn't seem real.

Clarity

The most important thing to remember when communicating in business is to be clear. If the recipient is left with more questions than answers, the message has failed. Clarity can only be attained by an in-depth familiarity with the intended message, the selected medium, and the means of transmission. If you don't have a firm grasp on these aspects, your message won't resonate as well.

Consistency

Consider reading a book that unexpectedly transitions from a solemn historical romance to a spooky screwball comedy before concluding with a high-brow literary study. Any reader would be confused and annoyed by such inconsistencies. When communicating in business, it's very important to keep your tone, voice, and content consistent. While variations on a theme might add interest, the fundamental message needs to be consistent.

Relevancy

Each of your communications must be consistent with what has come before it and what will come next without detracting from the central value proposition. Make sure that everything makes sense in a business context. For example, a blog post about the NBA player's free throw record accompanied by an inbound marketing press conference is bewildering. Always make sure your business writing makes sense in context.

Empathy

Empathy is widely regarded as one of the most important qualities in a leader. Allowing employees to know that you hear and understand how they feel makes them feel heard and respected. A recent survey indicated that despite its significance, 92% of respondents believe empathy is underrated, revealing its unrealized potential (Businessolver, n.d.). Increase understanding and foster a culture of productivity by training yourself to respond with empathy.

Targeting

If you really want to connect with your target audience, you need to put some thought into who your audience is. Audience awareness is the foundation for clarity, comprehensiveness, and objectivity. Focus your message on the specific needs of that audience. When you write to a company's SVP, you don't write like you would to a coworker or a client. Your audience's age, degree of education, and desired outcomes should all be reflected in your writing. This can be accomplished by research and taking the reader's position into account.

Transparency

Accessibility is a good way to talk to people. It's important to be present, visible, and accessible beyond only through emails and official statements. Your leadership style is communicated to those around you through your consistent and predictable visibility. People can't connect with you unless they have a sense of who you are. Take part in conversations with all relevant parties, especially in trying times.

Flexibility

The Economist Intelligence Unit found that conflicts over communication styles were the most often mentioned reason of poor communication, which in turn can lead to more serious concerns including priority confusion and emotional strain (McKenzie & Qazi, 1983).

Understanding how you are regarded and how you interact with colleagues requires you to know what kind of leader you are. If you're an effective leader, you probably have a well-defined goal in mind and arrange the team to maximize the likelihood of reaching that goal. Although this strategy works well for some people, those who like greater independence in their work may be disappointed. Knowing how to adapt your communication style to the individual needs of your audience is crucial for gaining buy-in from people and advancing your organization's goals.

Types of Communication and How They Affect People

Understanding how different team members talk to each other is a big part of building trust within the group. An increased capacity for trust and cooperation is just one byproduct of this comprehension. If a leader takes the time to learn the ins and outs of his or her team's communication style, they may be able to make better, faster decisions. With this understanding, you can adjust your approach to communication to meet the needs of your team members and foster an atmosphere of cooperation and harmony.

There is a significant difference between each of the five communication styles, in contrast to other communication preferences such as DiSC and the Enneagram. As a general rule, some methods of expression are more productive than others.

Assertive

The hallmark of an assertive communicator is a focus on clarity and directness that avoids being aggressive or condescending. Confidence in your own needs and the ability to listen attentively to those of others are at the heart of an assertive communication style, which strikes the fine balance necessary for reaching agreements and settling differences.

Even when the stakes are high, this method of expression stays consistent. Assertive communicators retain an enthusiastic, constructive, and measured approach, focused on solutions. They keep their cool under pressure and prioritize honest communication. While working together, they listen carefully to others and protect their own ideas and beliefs.

The use of "I" phrases, which encourages individual accountability, is a hallmark of assertive speech. For instance, instead of accusing someone, you could say something like, "I think you could have been nicer to our client." Instead of using vague terms like "could," "should," or "maybe," people who are confident in their communication skills prefer to state their intentions explicitly. They make unequivocal declarations of their goals rather than hesitatingly presenting tentative choices; for example, they would state, "I am going to work on this part of the project," rather than expressing any form of uncertainty.

Aggressive

If you're determined to win and think your view is more important than that of your coworkers, managers, or clients, you may be communicating in an aggressive way. This style is characterized by an imperious attitude that frequently leaves others feeling harassed, ignored, and underappreciated.

People who are overly dominant in conversation and who are only interested in advancing their own point of view often silence those who disagree with them. The strong tone used has a chilling effect on teamwork and might cause individuals to feel defensive about voicing their thoughts.

Even though aggressive communicators seem sure of themselves, they lack the important skill of active listening, which is something confident communicators have. When someone don't care about how their words make others feel, it shows in their tone of voice and dilutes the importance of what they're saying. Aggressive communicators risk turning off their listeners regardless of how valid their views may be.

When someone is being aggressive, their body language becomes aggressive as well. This can include aggressive hand gestures, unfriendly facial expressions, and unwelcome intrusions into personal space. This manner discourages open discussion and hinders progress on group projects. When compared to assertive communication, an aggressive approach fails to take into account the feelings and thoughts of others, which can lead to tense relationships within a team and decreased productivity.

Passive Communication

A passive communicator is one who submits and tries to please other people; they avoid confrontation and give in when others are more forceful or hostile. People who use this approach tend to back down from arguments whenever possible and let more forceful or aggressive traits shine through. Some people, who are more assertive, find that passive communicators are a pleasure to be around because of how accommodating they are.

This method of peacemaking, on the other hand, can plant the seeds of resentment. When they're at work, passive communicators risk being overshadowed and forgotten because they have a hard time making their own wants, needs, and views understood.

Passive communication might be a good strategy for dealing with a difficult or dominant customer, but it can backfire if you constantly put other people's needs before your own. This leads to miscommunication, which in turn causes burnout. Finding the right balance between meeting other people's wants and stating your own is important for developing a way of talking to others that leads to mutual respect and understanding.

Passive-Aggressive Communication

By cleverly combining parts of both passive and aggressive communication styles, passive-aggressive communication gives the impression of passivity while hiding anger and rage underneath. People who use this style seem calm and collected on the outside, but their true feelings are hidden. A storm of anger is building up underneath the surface, showing up in subtle but harmful ways like snark, gossip, spreading rumors, and talking down to others.

People who are passive-aggressive prefer to stay out of the spotlight and avoid direct conflict, in contrast to assertive communicators who voice their disagreements publicly. Even though they behave in a sneaky way, the harmful effects are just as bad, if not worse than the effects of being rude. Their resentment spreads like a virus, making everyone on the team doubtful and unhappy. If discovered, their coworkers may be reluctant to work with them due to the potential fallout, leading to an unproductive and disruptive work atmosphere. A healthy and open work environment can only be achieved by shedding light on the complexities of passive-aggressive communication.

Manipulative Communication

The covert, manipulative communication approach shapes results by trickery and deceit. At first evasive, people using this approach deftly avoid communicating their actual feelings and intentions. Until their aims are met—if they are ever revealed—manipulative communicators are masters at keeping people in the dark about their true intentions.

In contrast to aggressive communicators, who aren't afraid to say what they want, manipulative communicators will use deceit to get what they want. As master manipulators, they know that the key to success is keeping their genuine intentions hidden under a web of ambiguity.

There may be some immediate benefits for manipulative communicators, but I seriously doubt that this approach will work in the long run. Once teammates figure out the deception, it can lead to distrust and resentment, which in turn can ruin relationships on the job. Colleagues may desist from working with manipulative persons if they feel uncomfortable working with them, which is a natural reaction. If we want to build a trusting and open workplace, we must learn to recognize the subtle signs of manipulative communication.

Change Your Communication Style for Diverse Audiences

Learning to adapt your message based on who you're speaking to is a crucial skill for good communicators. This sophisticated ability requires you to use a variety of tactics to guarantee that your message resounds precisely. The key to quickly captivating your audience and creating a relationship that produces the best outcomes is to expertly customize your approach.

Take into account things like the audience's background, tastes, and communication style when using this customized communication strategy. With careful planning and execution, this method not only allows for a more in-depth interaction, but it also establishes the groundwork for fruitful results in a variety of communication contexts.

Understand Your Target Audience

When you're in business, you'll have to talk to plenty of different people. This could involve interacting with government or regulatory bodies, marketing, socializing, staff meetings, customer and supplier meetings, disciplinary procedures, and so on.

No matter the context, the aim of your communication is to get your point across as clearly and concisely as possible. It is acceptable to employ business language and principles when presenting your concept to a group of coworkers. If you're presenting to a large group of prospective clients though, this may not work.

Therefore, it is essential to know your audience inside and out so that you can tailor your message and way of speaking to their requirements.

Goals of Communication

It's important to know why you're communicating because that will help you craft your message. With this information on hand, you can use it to foresee how the target audience will respond and adjust your message, tone, and media accordingly.

For instance, are you informing clients of a brand shift or trying to sell them new products through your correspondence? The content, tone, and channel of your messages will vary greatly depending on your goal.

Also, the tone and style of communication you use when addressing stakeholders or consumers on behalf of your company during a crisis will differ greatly from those you use when wishing them a Merry Christmas or Happy Holiday. So, remembering your goals will guide you in determining the tone and the most effective way to communicate with your audience.

Using Several Mediums for Communication

For successful corporate communication, it is equally important to consider the medium you are employing. Salespeople and relationship managers, for instance, might read a completely different script when conducting phone due diligence checks with customers than when tweeting about your newest product launch.

So, divide your target audience into smaller groups and consider the methods they're likely to use for communication. A restaurant could effectively remind customers of their upcoming reservations by sending them a text message. On the other hand, business-to-business (B2B) organizations often prefer to communicate with clients using email and telephone.

Modify Your Delivery

The term "delivery" refers to the process of expressing yourself verbally, nonverbally, and visually. Changing your delivery means changing your speed, volume, tone, body language, eye contact, and slides so that they fit the listeners and the situation.

If you are addressing a diverse and huge crowd, for instance, it may be beneficial to talk more slowly and confidently, make more eye contact and gestures, and utilize colorful and easy slides. A more intimate and familiar setting may call for a more conversational tone, a faster pace of speech, fewer hand gestures and less eye contact, and more comprehensive and engaging visual aids.

Actively Listening and Analyzing Feedback

Leadership success hinges on the ability to listen attentively and analyze input proficiently. When you listen actively, you put yourself in the speaker's shoes and try to understand not only what they're saying but also their feelings and goals. It helps teams develop a culture of mutual understanding, trust, and open dialogue. Leaders that practice active listening are better able to understand their teams' thoughts, feelings, and goals, which in turn fosters a leadership style that is more collaborative and empathic.

By providing useful context and commentary, feedback processing enhances active listening. It means looking at feedback objectively, finding patterns, and changing approaches based on those patterns. To improve team performance, leaders can adapt their strategies, take the initiative to solve problems, and take advantage of this dynamic process.

Improved Understanding

By actively listening to their teams, leaders can gain a deeper understanding of their employees' thoughts, feelings, and challenges. When leaders have a better grasp of the situation, they are better able to make decisions that serve the team's objectives.

Trust Development

People on a team feel more heard and appreciated when their leaders do the same. When everyone on the team knows their thoughts and input are valued, trust grows. A cohesive and effective team relies on trust.

Settlement of Disputes

Resolving disagreements can be as simple as practicing active listening. Leaders are better able to resolve disagreements and reach solutions that work for everyone when they have a firm grasp of the fundamental issues and concerns at play.

Engagement and Morale in the Workplace

Employee engagement and morale are both boosted when they see that their suggestions are being considered and implemented. Proactively seeking and acting upon feedback fosters an encouraging work environment where employees are encouraged to take initiative and have a personal stake in the company's success.

Ongoing Improvement

By actively listening and analyzing information, a feedback loop is established that guarantees an ongoing improvement cycle. Leaders may use real-time data to improve plans, policies, and communication, which helps the team and company grow and develop over time.

The Key to Powerful Communication

Crucial to strong leadership communication, active listening helps teams connect and understand each other. Everything that makes it up is broken down into the following:

Centering on the Speaker and What They Have to Say

When you listen actively, you focus only on what the speaker is saying. That is, to pay close attention to the speaker without interruption from your phone or other activities. In doing so, leaders show their listeners how much they appreciate their perspective.

Focusing on the Speaker's Nonverbal Communication

There are times when non-verbal clues say more than words ever could. A leader who is actively listening will keep an eye on the speaker's gestures, facial expressions, and body language. This all-encompassing method enhances comprehension by shedding light on the speaker's feelings and thoughts.

Establishing Rapport

A leader's goal when actively listening to their team members should be to establish rapport. To do this, it is necessary to comprehend not just the uttered words but also the feelings and goals conveyed by the speaker. If leaders take the time to recognize and validate these traits, they may build trust and connection with their team.

Responding Genuinely

The art of active listening is in being genuine. When leaders respond with true empathy, it shows that they truly comprehend the speaker's point of view. Team members feel safe voicing their opinions and concerns because of this genuineness, which helps foster an environment of open and honest communication.

Accurately Processing Feedback and Navigating Conversations

Being able to listen attentively and digest feedback well are two skills necessary for effective leadership. Let's take a closer look at the key elements:

Paying Attention While Listening and Not Cutting Off: The first step in processing feedback is to listen carefully. In order to give each speaker a chance to finish their thought, leaders control the impulse to cut them off. Leaders keep an eye on their own emotional reactions to make sure they're measured and can lead to productive conversations.

Clarifying: To make sure the feedback they get is understood correctly, leaders always ask for clarification. By asking clarifying questions and restating important concepts, they help to establish a common ground. By taking the time to explain things more clearly, you show that you care about getting other people's points of view and avoiding miscommunication.

Staying in Touch: Feedback is not a one-and-done deal; active leaders get that. To evaluate the effect of earlier comments and to investigate any new ideas or worries, they start follow-up conversations. An atmosphere of free communication is fostered, and a culture of continual improvement is advanced through this mutual dialogue.

Giving Your Own Feedback: Being a leader is a two-way street. Leaders who are great at taking criticism well also have insightful things to say. This back-and-forth helps create an environment where people are more likely to work together, while also removing obstacles to communication and laying the groundwork for a feedback culture.

Expression Through Body Language

The ability to express oneself nonverbally is a key component of effective communication. Nonverbal communication can take many forms, including but not limited to the use of hand gestures and facial expressions, eye contact (or lack thereof), closeness, and other physical signals.

Our body language conveys a great deal of information. Some studies have even shown that nonverbal communication accounts for four times as much as verbal communication; in other words, 80% of human communication is nonverbal, with only 20% being expressed through words (Cherry, 2023).

In our daily interactions with others, we pick up on countless nonverbal clues and behaviors, such as body language, facial expressions, eye contact, gestures, and vocal intonation. Everything we do with our hair and how we shake hands is a form of nonverbal communication that says a lot about us and influences the way we interact with others.

Different Kinds of Body Language Expressions

There has been an abundance of studies on the many forms, impacts, and manifestations of nonverbal communication and behavior. Let's take a look at some kinds of non-verbal communications:

Facial Expressions

When people smile, frown, or make any number of other facial expressions, they are expressing a great deal of information that would not be possible through words alone. When we first meet someone, our perceptions are already colored by their looks, long before any words are exchanged. Expressions of joy, grief, rage, and terror are more or less the same throughout cultures, despite the fact that nonverbal communication is subject to cultural subtleties. One of the most important skills for communicating effectively in a variety of contexts is the capacity to read and react to nonverbal signs, such as expressions and gestures, on people's faces.

Gazing/Eye Movements

The nonverbal signs conveyed by eye gaze—which includes staring, blinking, and looking—are essential to effective communication. The blinking rate and pupil dilation can be accelerated when a person is in the presence of items or people that they enjoy.

Moods like hostility, attention, and attraction can be seen in the eyes. Also, people typically use eye-look indicators to determine whether someone is being honest or not. Mainly, people look at those who maintain continuous eye contact and act truthfully and trustworthy when they greet them. On the flip side, people tend to be suspicious of dishonesty when they notice that someone can't keep their eyes on the person they're talking to.

Posture

When it comes to communicating nonverbal cues, posture and body language are kings. According to Julius Fast's book *Body Language*, the field of body language analysis has been greatly exaggerated in the media, especially when it comes to the deciphering of protective postures like arm-crossing and leg-crossing, which rose to prominence in the 1970s (Cherry, 2023).

Be that as it may, there is a great deal of intricacy involved in interpreting nonverbal clues, such as body language, which can provide light on attitudes and emotions. Most people misunderstand the subtlety and ambiguity of body language, which goes against popular belief. To fully understand these nonverbal cues, you need a complex view that takes into account many factors and avoids making too many broad assumptions.

Using Gestures

Without the need for words, gestures—defined as deliberate motions and signals—provide a substantial form of communication. The most basic hand motions, like raising one's hand in a greeting or pointing, are understood all over the world. Yet, there are cultural undertones to certain gestures. The "V" sign means victory or peace in the US but is insulting in some places (such as the UK and Australia); this is just one example.

Some judges even prohibit specific gestures in court because of the great influence they can have on jurors' verdicts. This is all because of how crucial nonverbal communication is, particularly through gestures. As an example, a lawyer might look at their watch to show that they are bored with the other side's argument, or they could roll their eyes while a witness is testifying to undermine their credibility. Perceptions and interactions are greatly influenced by these nonverbal clues.

Paralinguistics

Tone, volume, inflection, and pitch are all aspects of vocal communication that fall under the umbrella of paralinguistics. It is remarkable how much of an effect the pitch of the voice has on the meaning of a phrase. When you say something out loud with conviction, people may see it as an expression of approval and excitement, but when you speak slowly, they could come across as disapproval or a lack of interest. This part of nonverbal conversation shows how the quality of your voice can change how you understand what someone is saying.

Haptics

Nonverbal cues such as haptics—the power of touch to express feelings like familiarity, pity, and affection—are vital in relationships with others. People with better social standing tend to be more intrusive and persistent in their invasions of personal space than those with lesser social standing. The way men and women use physical touch differs; men may use it to exert dominance and control, while women use it to show caring and nurturing. Some studies, like the famous monkey study by Harry Harlow, show how important touch is for growth and social interaction in the early years of life (Cherry, 2023).

Physical Representation

One way people express themselves nonverbally is by their appearance, which includes their clothes, hairdos, and other visual aspects. According to studies in color psychology, differing colors can influence people's emotional states, which in turn affect their body language and how they perceive the world (Webinopoly, n.d.).

The importance of first impressions is highlighted by the fact that people make snap judgments about others based on their looks.

It is important to dress professionally for interviews, as this reflects well on the candidate. Researchers have found a link between being attractive and better wages and other benefits. This shows how society affects how people make decisions (Dilmaghani, 2020). People from different cultural backgrounds have different ideas about what it means to be attractive. Some African cultures value full-figured bodies as symbols of health, prosperity, and social standing, whereas Western societies may place a premium on thinness.

Getting Past Communication Problems

It takes flexibility and sensitivity to overcome communication difficulties. Successful leaders know how to establish an atmosphere that encourages open dialogue, teamwork, and long-term achievement. Overcoming obstacles is an essential part of successfully navigating the challenging landscape of leadership communication. Let's explore the details of each part:

Listening Attentively

A key component in removing obstacles to communication is active listening. To create a space where everyone feels heard and appreciated, leaders work on mastering the art of genuine understanding.

Understanding and Considering Culture

Cultural differences affect how people talk to each other at work. Leaders that put in the time and effort to learn about other cultures are better able to bridge gaps in understanding and establish an environment that welcomes and celebrates diversity.

Boosting Non-Speech Expression

In many cases, non-verbal clues are more informative than words themselves. In order to convey the right messages, leaders work to perfect their non-verbal cues, such as their facial expressions and body language.

Moving Past Emotional Obstacles

Feelings get in the way of talking things out. In order to overcome emotional barriers, leaders create a safe space for their team members to share their thoughts, feelings, and opinions.

Prompt Exchange of Information

Unclear communication leads to a climate of mistrust. In order to foster a culture of dependability and reduce the likelihood of misunderstandings, leaders place a premium on timely communication.

Conflict Management

Communication flow can be disrupted by conflicts. Leaders are masters at conflict management because they promote an environment of open communication, mediate disagreements, and encourage teamwork in finding solutions.

Resolving Physical Obstacles

Physical obstacles, including working remotely or having an awkward workplace arrangement, might make it hard to communicate. Leaders take action to close these gaps, using technology and careful design to make things more accessible.

Fostering Confidence and Openness

The foundation of good communication is trust. Leaders build trust by setting a good example themselves and being consistent in what they do. This encourages team members to feel comfortable voicing their opinions.

Embracing Criticism

Establishing a feedback culture is something that leaders actively promote. Leaders show humility and a desire to grow continuously by listening to feedback, which creates an environment where people are more likely to proactively work to overcome communication obstacles.

An Interactive Element: Practicing Active Listening Skills

Take a look at this detailed exercise to see how active listening might benefit you.

Exercise: "So What I Heard is..."

1. Pick a video—ideally a TED talk from YouTube—to interact with on social media.

2. Turn off the subtitles and mute the video so you can read the crowd and speaker's body language.

3. Observe the speaker's body language to determine their topic, tone, and level of rapport with the audience.

4. Unmute the video but don't turn on the subtitles.

5. Pay rapt attention to what the speaker is saying and how they are saying it.

6. Take a short break from the video every now and then and repeat what you've heard. Come up with some questions you'd want to ask the speaker.

7. Pay attention to how your questions fit in with the presenter's progression. Was the speaker able to cover what you were hoping to hear? Through this thought, you can see that you clearly understand how to listen actively.

Active listening is an art form, and this exercise will help you hone your ability to understand subtleties in spoken language. Perfecting the art of active listening takes time and effort, but the payoff is richer relationships and deeper conversations in your personal and professional life.

Chapter 4:

The Role of Communication in Leadership

To effectively communicate, we must realize that we are all different in the way we perceive the world and use this understanding as a guide to our communication with others.
—Tony Robbins

The value of communication in today's ever-changing leadership environment is paramount. It's more than just talking; it's the driving factor behind good leadership. In this chapter, we recognize the various perspectives that people have by drawing on Tony Robbins' deep wisdom.

Proceeding from the ground up, we intend to explore the far-reaching effects of communication on the efficacy of leadership in this chapter. This is more of an interactive experience than a course of action; it's a guide for navigating the complexity of leadership.

This chapter will go deep into the topic at hand, illuminating the ways in which good communication motivates, brings people together, and settles disputes. This is more than just an adventure; it's a chance to become an expert communicator in a leadership role, where your words have the power to move people.

In this quest for knowledge, let us delve into the complex relationships between leadership and communication. Throughout this course, you will learn how to communicate effectively as a leader and how to put that knowledge to use in your own leadership development.

Business Leadership: How does Communication Matter?

Leaders have always been those who inspire their followers to better themselves and reach their full potential. Great leaders are able to accomplish this because they are skilled communicators. Many great leaders, like Abraham Lincoln, have been excellent communicators. In fact, it has been said that there is a correlation between strong leadership and good communication skills. Consequently, being able to communicate effectively is crucial for any leader who aspires to achieve success. Therefore, how does effective communication factor into leadership?

Effective leaders are able to articulate their team's objectives in a way that everyone can understand. As an added bonus, it helps in figuring out what the team members want and how to address their concerns. The ability to communicate effectively also helps leaders build trusting relationships with their staff, which in turn boosts efficiency and output. So, it's clear that being able to communicate well is a key part of being a leader.

Encouraging and Uplifting Others

The words you choose to use as a leader may motivate your team like no other. You motivate other people to perform at their highest level when you show unfaltering dedication, share an inspiring vision, and celebrate successes. When you motivate people, you're not merely pushing them; you're kindling a fire that drives them to achieve greatness.

Developing Trust

Leadership is based on trust. One way to establish trust in a team is to communicate with them in an open, honest, and consistent manner. With trust, people feel more comfortable speaking their minds, taking calculated risks, and connecting with one another. To strengthen that trust, a leader's actions should match their words.

Encouraging Teamwork

Building bridges and fostering collaboration are two outcomes of effective communication. Facilitating cross-functional discussions, fostering varied viewpoints, and actively listening to others all contribute to an atmosphere where ideas may thrive. Working together as a team isn't enough; true collaboration involves tapping into everyone's knowledge and expertise to tackle difficult problems.

Empowering the Team

Efficient teams accomplish great things. The best way for a leader to empower their team is to lay out specific goals, assign specific responsibilities, and promote an environment of autonomy. Team members are more likely to take initiative, own their work, and make significant contributions when there is clear and consistent communication about expectations and goals. Embracing autonomy promotes creativity and adaptability.

Getting Everyone on the Same Page

Eloquence isn't everything when it comes to leadership communication; alignment is. Defining and communicating the organization's purpose, long-term plans, and common objectives is essential. When everyone is on the same page, they can work together to reach their goal. You must ensure that the compass remains pointed in the correct direction at all times as a leader.

Resolving Conflicts and Mediating

When it comes to the complex world of leadership, two crucial areas where good communication is key are mediation and dispute resolution. The foundation of this strategy is a thorough familiarity with the issues raised by all sides of the dispute. In this pivotal moment, active listening—an anchor of good communication—takes center stage, laying the groundwork for solutions that go beyond peacemaking and compromise.

Building trust, getting support, and starting an open conversation are just a few of the many ways that good communication can help solve conflicts. These are not just necessary but catalytic factors; without them, disagreements can quickly turn into long-term problems.

Leaders use a sophisticated set of communication abilities that go beyond the basics when resolving conflicts. Remaining composed and collected while speaking can be a powerful strategy for building an atmosphere that is favorable to productive conversations. To maintain a level playing field, it's important to listen to all sides of a disagreement and consider their arguments.

Successful communicators skillfully maneuver through complex conflict situations by utilizing the armory of strategies outlined in the previous chapter. A combination of empathy, clarity, and boldness can steer conversations in the direction of cooperative solutions. The power of communication to bring about change is consistently emphasized as we explore the complex domains of mediation and conflict resolution. Beyond its role as a stress management tool, it helps foster an environment where employees can work together productively, transforming disagreements into opportunities for learning and advancement.

Primary Challenges to Conflict Resolution

Whether it's with their subordinates, customers, suppliers, coworkers, or even on a more personal level, managers wind up devoting a lot of time to mediating workplace conflicts. On top of that, research shows that conflicts have significant direct and indirect costs that cut into your profits (Crestcom, 2020). No matter which of the several approaches to dispute resolution professionals recommend you try, you're bound to encounter the same old problems. A quick rundown of the challenges to dispute settlement follows.

Playing Defense

Getting defensive when confronted with an argument is a normal human response. However, becoming defensive is a certain way of "adding fuel to the fire." How frustrating! Taking the defensive stance will not only make the other person angrier, but it will also prevent you from hearing and comprehending their point of view. Basically, it prevents the kind of honest, reciprocal dialogue that is essential for finding a workable solution. Try not to get defensive and instead focus on hearing the other person out. If you feel the need, ask them for additional information and their thoughts on the matter.

Skipping Over the Subject as Unimportant

Do either of these ring a bell?

"You're going overboard with this."

"That is not how you should be feeling."

If someone approaches you with a problem and is expressing their displeasure in the manners shown above, it shows that you don't consider the issue significant. They want it to matter to you; therefore, you should make it a priority. Feelings are just information; they are not right or wrong. This is something you must remember. Saying anything like, "You shouldn't be feeling that way," is completely inappropriate.

Rather than brushing off their emotions, try to understand what is triggering them. You can accomplish this by politely requesting more information and then restating what you have just heard. By doing so, you can confirm that you have heard them and fully get their point of view on the matter. Keep in mind that the point is not to judge their sentiments and viewpoints as right or wrong, but to comprehend the origin of the disagreement.

Judging Without Facts

Our minds have evolved to make rapid, complicated decisions based on our experiences, so this is really challenging. When it came to resolving conflicts in our daily lives, this wasn't so useful, but it was while we were hunting and gathering for food in ancient times.

When a disagreement involves us directly, our defensiveness may cause us to jump to conclusions. It can also happen while you're trying to resolve a dispute, like when two coworkers are at odds with each other. Be careful not to assume anything before you hear all sides of the argument.

Putting off making a decision until you've heard opposing arguments is one way to avoid jumping to conclusions, which isn't easy. If there are eyewitnesses to the dispute, it could be wise to have them weigh in on the story as well.

Ignoring What Others Have to Say

Everyone here is guilty of the usual problem of preoccupying themselves with plotting their response rather than actually listening. The issue, like many other obstacles, is that we fail to listen to the other person and do not give ourselves the opportunity to comprehend their point of view. When people actively listen to one another during tense situations, it helps everyone involved to calm down, show less aggression, and show respect for one another.

Get yourself to stop thinking about what you're going to say and just listen instead. You must do this for two reasons: First, it shows the other party that you are paying attention; and second, it ensures that you have fully grasped what they are expressing.

A Lack of Social Empathy

In conflict situations, especially when one party is clearly at fault, some of us simply have a harder time empathizing with the other. Having compassion for another person, however, is unrelated to judging their rightness or wrongness. By doing so, you are merely letting the other person know that you have listened to their perspective and empathize with their feelings.

Realize that you understand their feelings are more important than giving them a long speech when you want to demonstrate empathy. Your response could sound like this: "I can see that you're probably wondering, 'Why should I bother?' To whom does it really matter? Is that how you're feeling?" Doing so is an excellent approach to show that you understand and empathize with the other person, regardless of how you may be feeling emotionally.

No Self-Control

There are times when everything goes off the rails and the argument gets worse. It seems like everyone is getting angrier and raising their voices, going into "attack mode." In this particular situation, you will also start to feel a loss of control. But you need to keep your composure and not lose your temper under any circumstances. When you're trying to solve a problem, this is probably the worst thing you could do.

Take a moment to consider your next move before speaking or doing anything. What kind of impact will this have on the situation? Talking softly and calmly will help you and those around you relax. Make sure your comments are factual and free of bias, and foster an environment where people feel comfortable expressing their thoughts freely. Hopefully, by following these steps, you can de-escalate the situation and prevent yourself from adding gasoline to the fire. This will allow everyone involved to move forward with finding a settlement.

Remember that there is no guarantee that every disagreement will end in a win-win situation. We may, however, make use of whatever is available to us to manage conflict and find mutually agreeable solutions, so that everyone involved feels heard and respected. Ultimately, isn't that what we all desire?

Constructive Criticism: A Major Challenge

When it comes to providing constructive criticism, how comfortable are you? If you feel like your abilities could be improved, you certainly aren't alone. I know it sounds crazy, but just 14.5 percent of managers really feel that they're good at providing constructive criticism (Brower & Dvorak, 2019). Mastering the art of constructive criticism without demoralizing a coworker requires honesty and balance, which can be challenging even when one has good intentions.

Keeping It Real While Being Polite

The art of providing constructive criticism is subtle and complex, requiring a balance of directness and sensitivity. Leaders move with caution, making sure their criticism is constructive without being overly critical. The trick is to keep the receiver's spirits up and encourage their development while providing insights that motivate improvement.

Encouraging Positive Two-Way Conversations

A dynamic interaction is the pinnacle of communication. By encouraging a positive two-way conversation, good communication goes beyond monologue when providing constructive criticism. It promotes open communication so that the other person feels comfortable giving their opinion and asking for more information. When people are able to provide and receive criticism in this way, it fosters an environment where everyone is always striving to do better.

Precision, Directness, and Executability

The key to providing meaningful constructive criticism is effective communication. It needs to be simple to understand, detailed enough to identify problem areas, and actionable enough to lay out a plan for fixing those problems. The key is to explain what went wrong and how to fix it, fostering a growth-oriented mindset.

Tips on How to Give Constructive Criticism

Knowing how to offer constructive criticism is the first step in effective communication. Here's a detailed outline of what to do while providing criticism remotely:

- Avoid using blurred words like "always" or "never" and instead be explicit by providing examples. Give detailed examples of the thing or behavior you want to change.

- If you want your feedback to stick with the receiver, use examples from their own experience to back up your claims.

- Give advice that people can actually use: Make suggestions for how things can be better without telling them how to fix it.

- After hearing your criticism, have the person think about how they might solve the problem on their own.

- Pay attention to what's happening, not who's doing it.

- Stay focused on the situation instead of the person to avoid accusatory responses.

- Thinking of the other person as someone you greatly admire will help you stay positive and focused on finding a solution.

- Find a happy medium: While providing constructive criticism, be sure to also compliment the person on their strengths and achievements.

- Maintaining a steady equilibrium promotes an openness to criticism.

- Recognize progress: When the individual takes your suggestions into consideration and makes adjustments, it's important to recognize their hard work and the beneficial changes they've achieved.

- Acknowledging progress highlights the significance of productive dialogue.

A Culture of Open Communication

Successful leaders know that an open-door policy, transparent team divisions, and the elimination of barriers are the cornerstones of a healthy work environment. Tragically, though, many leaders fail to take these important steps, which causes major problems with team communication.

Not only do these problems make it harder to get things done on a daily basis, but they also hurt the leadership's overall effectiveness and success. Although leaders face these obstacles, there are things they can do right now to strengthen their communication methods. A more productive and peaceful workplace can be achieved when leaders put an emphasis on open communication and use collaborative strategies.

When it comes to the workplace, having open communication is absolutely necessary. A lack of open conversation in the workplace can cause a number of problems. For example, 43% of business leaders surveyed for the State of Business Communication study say that bad communication makes their teams less productive (Grammarly Business, 2023). Missing or being late for tasks is one of the worst things that can happen when people don't talk to each other or understand each other. Poor communication also affects the company's bottom line, according to 38% (Grammarly Business, 2023).

When it comes to helping your teams improve their communication skills, there is no one best approach. One way to encourage open conversation in your business is to do any of the following:

Create a Respectful Culture

Create a work environment that promotes open communication and respects different points of view. Foster an environment of mutual respect by making it safe for employees to speak their minds without worrying about retaliation.

Encourage Active Listening

Encourage your teams to practice active listening by teaching them to hear and comprehend one another's points of view without passing judgment. Overall, team connection is improved by making sure that everyone feels like they are being heard.

Put Teamwork Resources to Use

Encourage free flow of information by means of group work applications, such as intranets, message platforms, or project management software. These technologies make it easier for team members to share information, work together on tasks, and provide feedback.

Schedule Regular Meetings

Keep the lines of communication open by holding regular team meetings. To keep the lines of communication open regarding current projects or difficulties, encourage staff to report progress, ask questions, and provide comments.

Show the Way

The tone is set by leadership. Leaders should be models of open communication by talking to their teams, listening to what they have to say, and accepting criticism with open arms.

Offer Ways for Feedback

Set up official avenues for comments, recommendations, or worries. Foster an environment that welcomes feedback by encouraging employees to use these channels and promising to give their views careful consideration.

Set Up Team-Building Exercises

Plan team-building events like brainstorming or group discussions, to help people talk to each other freely, trust each other, and share their ideas.

Put an Open-Door Policy in Place

Make sure that supervisors can be reached at all times by instituting an open-door policy. This will encourage employees to share their thoughts and concerns with them.

Deliver Communication Abilities Training

Develop courses that teach people how to communicate effectively, including how to listen actively, resolve conflicts, and be more aggressive. Improving these skills enables workers to converse more fluently.

Praise Openness and Honesty

Honest and open conversation should be praised and rewarded. Recognizing these traits encourages people to be more open and honest, which is crucial in today's world.

Simplify Your Expressions

Make sure everyone on the team can understand you by staying away from any jargon or complicated language. When everyone in the team is using the same, simple language, everyone can understand each other better.

Leadership Through the Use of Storytelling

Effective leadership that uses stories to get people on board is a big part of getting people to work harder and be more engaged in their jobs. As an acquired skill, it enables leaders to inspire their teams by sharing their vision and encouraging others to suspend their views in favor of fresh ideas.

Leadership that is characterized by excellent storytelling abilities is more likely to attract top talent, has better success in dealing with the media, and fosters stronger relationships, all of which contribute to increased fundraising and fruitful business agreements, according to Virtual Speech (MAYHEW, 2021).

The leader must reflect on their own experiences and be candid about issues that their staff can relate to in order to include storytelling in their leadership style. One way leaders may motivate their teams and foster a shared vision is by openly discussing the challenges they overcame.

Build Credibility

Leaders can build credibility through the use of storytelling. As a leader, showing your team members some humanity through sharing personal or company stories is a great way to build trust and authenticity.

Company-Wide Mentality Change

Engaging stories can change the way people think at work. By sharing stories about problems and solutions, leaders can change how their teams see and deal with problems, which can make the organization's culture more resilient and flexible.

Setting up Facts and Feelings

If a leader wants to inspire and motivate their team, they need to create a story that combines facts and emotions in a strategic way. Leaders can get their message across and guide their teams toward shared goals by connecting facts with emotions that people can relate to.

Turning Numbers into Powerful Goals

For the most part, leaders work with numbers and facts that are hard to understand. The power of storytelling enables people to transform these abstract numbers into captivating mental pictures of their goals. While leading a team, it's important for leaders to use stories to break down difficult ideas and help their followers see the bigger picture.

Raising Morale on the Team

Motivational storytelling has a lot of clout. Leaders have the power to inspire their teams by creating stories that speak to their hopes, beliefs, and values. When delivered well, a narrative can motivate people to work together toward a common goal.

Interactive Part

Role-playing games are great for helping teams improve their ability to communicate and work together to solve problems. Let's look at some situations that can help people who want to be leaders practice talking to people clearly:

1. A Disagreement at Work Situation

- Participants: Put your team members into pairs.

- Let's say that two coworkers have different ideas about how to approach a job. One wants to stick to a conservative, tried-and-true approach, while the other wants to try something new.

- Role-playing: Each pair becomes one of the two coworkers. Promote active listening, understanding, and helpful conversation. Finding a middle ground or an answer that works for both sides is the goal.

- Key Points: Listening actively, negotiating, and finding a middle ground.

2. A Conflict Scenario in Customer Service

- Participants: Break into smaller groups.

- Case: Participants pretend to be customer service reps who have to deal with angry customers. The customers are upset about a broken product or bad service.

- Role-Play: Each team takes it in turn to respond to consumer concerns.

- Challenge: Stay calm, understanding, and focused on finding an answer. The participants have to figure out how to fix the problem while keeping the customer experience good.

- Learning Points: Calming down, understanding, and solving problems.

3. "Two Sides of the Story":

- Participants: Pair up those who took part.

- Scenario: Each pair picks a real-life problem that happens at work, like missing a deadline, not being able to communicate, or not having enough resources. The scenario calls for two actors, one portraying the employee and the other the manager.

- Role-Playing: Each player gets a chance to tell their own story. The learner is actively listening and asking questions to get more information. After that, they switch places.

- Learning Points: Listening, knowing, and taking other people's points of view.

4. The Peacemaker:

- Participants: One referee and two people who are arguing.

- Scenario: Make up a fake disagreement at work, like two team members fighting over who should get credit for a successful project.

- Role-Play: The mediator helps the two sides talk to each other. Assist in finding common ground, lead the conversation, and encourage respectful communication.

- Learning Points: How to be fair, how to mediate, and how to solve conflicts.

Keep in mind that these exercises are more than just role-playing; they're a chance to work on your listening, empathy, and communication skills. As a leader, learning these skills will help you handle disagreements better and build teams that work better together.

Chapter 5:

The Ladder to Leadership Success

"Success usually comes to those who are too busy to be looking for it."
—Henry David Thoreau

Success in today's fast-paced job market typically comes to those who are actively working toward a goal rather than sitting on the sidelines, hoping for the best. These wise words by Henry David Thoreau set the tone for what we will be talking about in this chapter. This chapter discusses the details of networking and personal branding, two important factors that determine how far you can go in your job.

Standing out is of the utmost importance in today's cutthroat professional world. Insights that equip you to negotiate the intricacies of deliberate career planning are offered by this vibrant companion, which is more than just an educational conversation. As we begin this chapter, try to see it as more than just an exploration—it's a tangible roadmap with steps you can actually follow.

If you want to be a leader, you need to know how to network and build your personal brand. This chapter delves into these strategies, equipping you with the knowledge and self-assurance to chart your own course to leadership stardom. Come along as we uncover the keys to turning your career dreams into reality through an in-depth examination of personal branding and networking.

Building Relationships and Networking

While networking is a great investment in your professional future, it isn't always easy. Finding the correct people to talk to at the company you're interested in is just half the battle; you also have to find the nerve to approach those individuals. If you're an introvert or a busy company leader, don't worry—there are plenty of methods to start networking tomorrow without leaving your house.

Networking Online

One of the best things about online networking is how easy it is to gather a community of valuable people. Of course, you'll still require a solid plan, as is the case with any type of networking. For successful internet networking, remember these tips.

Picking Appropriate Digital Networking Spaces

Careful platform selection is an integral part of developing a winning online networking strategy. If you're looking to expand your network beyond LinkedIn, consider joining industry forums, Twitter, Slack groups, and Facebook groups. Join the growing number of online gatherings by setting up specific areas for networking and giving participants virtual meeting places. Using a variety of digital networking sites and being open to new trends can help you make more important connections and stay ahead of the online community for your industry.

Impart Knowledge and Make a Difference

People are eager to make connections with those they perceive as having the ability to assist them, as you will discover the more time and effort you put into networking. You can increase your value to other people by sharing your wisdom, experiences, and ideas. Helping out isn't required all the time, but it is important to make an effort to deliver helpful information. Make use of sites like LinkedIn to publish content relevant to your field and participate in forums where people ask questions about your area of expertise. You can show how helpful and knowledgeable you are by responding to messages asking for your opinion and taking part in podcasts or interviews.

Choose Quality Over Quantity

Although it's tempting to connect with influential people, you should be careful when selecting connections. Find other people in your field to learn from and network with. Get to know people who are already making a difference in your industry or who have ties to companies that interest you. Keep an open mind while interacting with people online; you never know who you might meet who could have a major influence on your professional life down the road. If someone else is willing to introduce you, take advantage of it. You never know who you could meet who could help you advance in your career.

Be Consistent

Being consistent is essential for thriving in networking. Set out time every week to interact with people online, read up on forum topics, and join in on conversations. Having a consistent online presence is essential for establishing meaningful connections. Keep your social media status updated with industry news and thoughts on a regular basis. The more active you are on social media, the more likely it is that people will notice you and be interested in connecting with you.

One-on-One Networking

Personal connections made through networking events are priceless when it comes to climbing the professional ladder. Personal encounters, as opposed to virtual ones, allow for the development of trust and a more indelible impression through the establishment of a true rapport. A great way to meet new people, share ideas, and look for ways to work together is to attend networking events and other industry gatherings. Your professional status will be strengthened by these interactions, which go beyond simple introductions and become a dynamic network.

What Are Your Networking Targets?

If you want to succeed in the complex world of business networking, you must first define your goals. Figure out if you want to advance in your current position, start a new one, or grow your business. The makeup of your network is influenced by these responses. Building relationships with vendors raises awareness of your business and networking with industry heavyweights might help you climb the corporate ladder. If you want to switch jobs, networking with high-ranking executives at potential employers is a good first step. It is important to remember that leaders are not limited to CEOs but can include anyone with significant knowledge and expertise in a certain field. Make the most of your company network's strategic influence by adjusting your ties to fit particular objectives.

Create an Impressive Opening

In the corporate world, an introduction is more than just a welcome; it should be a powerful sell. Even though acquaintances might turn into friends, the first meeting is crucial for establishing rapport. Stay away from salesmanship and instead focus on three positive aspects of yourself. Whether you're trying to increase exposure for your brand, boost sales, or climb the corporate ladder, it's important to make your goals clear when building your business network. By keeping these things in mind, you may have a more productive conversation and make more of an impression when networking.

Take the Lead with Confidence

Shyness isn't a big deal when it comes to professional networking. If you want to expand your professional network, you need to actively seek out people to connect with. Although most influential people in any field are kind and eager to make new contacts, it could be nerve-wracking to approach one and start a conversation.

Make sure you gather a list of everyone you would like to meet before going to industry gatherings. It is much easier to start conversations after doing some preliminary research, which provides useful topic starters. If you and your partner find that you both enjoy gardening, for instance, it would be a good idea to learn about some native species, including how to care for them. Prioritize sincere curiosity over professional knowledge.

Mastering eye contact is an important part of overcoming shyness and establishing trust in a professional network. To make it more comfortable, practice at home using a mirror. Maintaining eye contact during first encounters shows sincerity and reliability, which are crucial for building relationships.

Maintain Momentum

The next most important thing to do after making connections at a networking event that are relevant to your business or professional goals is to keep the conversation going. It would be impractical to depend on these leaders' and experts' memory given the number of connections they probably make.

Make use of the obtained contact details and start corresponding by email; at least for the time being, avoid using more personal methods of communication. With this strategy, you may show that you're still interested in the field and stay in touch with their professional networks. Your memorability and your ability to seize opportunities are both bolstered by a well-planned follow-up.

Establishing a Strong Bond with a Mentor

People who have mentors tend to do better in school, move up the corporate ladder more quickly, and report higher levels of job and life happiness. Even mentors reap the rewards. As the saying goes, "To teach is to learn twice." Despite these advantages, over half of working-age professionals do not have a mentor relationship, yet 76% of those same people think a mentor is critical to professional development (Horoszowski, 2020). Most of the time, folks just don't know where to look or how to start a conversation with a potential mentor. Here are some steps that might be useful.

Determine Your Needs and Goals

Prepare a list of all the things you want to do professionally. Do not forget to make them SMART (Specific, Measurable, Achievable, Relevant, and Time-Bound). After that, make a list of some of the most significant challenges you'll face in reaching those goals. You can narrow your search for a mentor by being as specific as this. Perhaps you need to hone your problem-solving abilities, broaden your professional network, or get the self-assurance to broach sensitive topics. Finding a mentor who can actually help you reach your goals requires first knowing where you want to go and then figuring out what obstacles stand in your way.

Make Use of People You Already Know as Mentors

One of the many potential sources of mentorship is your secondary network. If you look around, you might find more people who could be willing to mentor you than you imagine. This could be in your professional network, on LinkedIn, or even at conferences. The act of asking another person to be your mentor is itself a compliment. While they may say "No" because of time restrictions, asking is still an engaged and constructive action. Do not be afraid to set lofty goals; it is up to them to determine whether they have the time to devote to your mentoring. The trick is to ask for what you want without being afraid, knowing that what you want could help you advance in your career.

Asking for a Mentorship (Simplify It)

It could be uncomfortable to ask for a mentorship for the first time, especially if you've never been in that position before. Give in to the unease and risk being vulnerable while you're at it. A full-fledged mentoring relationship isn't necessary for the first request. If you want to learn more about their work and hobbies, start by asking to have a casual conversation. Prior to making a more formal request for mentorship, this methodical approach allows both sides to gauge compatibility and ease. It's best not to send a long email; keeping your request simple is key.

Accountability-Focused Mentorship Agreement

There should be some thought to formalizing your mentorship relationship after the first few discussions. Make a commitment to take action toward reaching your objectives on a monthly basis for the following half year. Get the mentorship off the ground with a simple one-page document that lays out the goals.

This agreement, however detailed it may appear, serves to clarify matters and align expectations between you and your mentor. Also, it helps keep meetings on track by outlining the agenda for each one. Make it clear that you appreciate their time and want to make the most of it when you approach the suggestion. Say something like,

"I was thinking about making a simple document with my three-month goals, commitments, and milestones. I can use this to hold myself to my word and get the most out of our discussions. Do you think that's something you can handle?"

A Mindset Designed for Mentorship

It takes more than just skill, knowledge, and perseverance to make it as a CEO or other top executive in a company; you also need the advice and encouragement of seasoned peers. By guiding them through the challenges of the corporate world and imparting wisdom and experience, mentors play an invaluable part in molding the leaders of tomorrow. Consider these five recommendations as we delve into the value of mentoring and its potential to help future company executives and CEOs reach their full potential.

1. Learning from the Experienced

Through mentoring relationships, leaders can have access to the extensive expertise of more seasoned colleagues. A mentor is someone who has been through the storm and come out on top, or at least had some experience with both. They can share important knowledge and wisdom that can help you make strategic decisions, solve problems, and be a better leader. Rising corporate executives and CEO hopefuls can speed up their careers by learning from the mistakes of others and making better decisions based on their own unique circumstances.

2. Promoting Development on Both a Personal and Employer Level

Both the mentee and the mentor benefit from the supportive atmosphere that mentorship offers. In their roles as trusted advisors, mentors provide mentees with support, direction, and criticism. In doing so, they help future leaders in assessing their own abilities and pinpointing where they can make the most progress in their careers and personal lives. Leaders in company and at the executive level can improve their abilities, get more knowledge, and develop the traits needed for effective leadership by receiving constructive criticism.

3. Growing Relationships and Networks

Among the many benefits of mentoring is the chance to meet new people and broaden one's network. Mentors typically have vast professional networks that can introduce mentees to new opportunities, collaborations, and partnerships. Executives and business owners can use these relationships to their advantage by increasing their visibility, consulting with subject-matter experts, and gaining access to resources that would be difficult to obtain otherwise. Mentorship provides an opportunity for business leaders to build connections that will have a lasting impact on their careers.

4. Mentorship as a Tool for Fostering Innovation

By bringing new ideas, viewpoints, and experiences to the table, mentors enrich leadership with innovation and creativity. Mentors inspire mentees to think creatively and independently by questioning established conventions and encouraging them to think beyond the box. In this dynamic, people are more likely to take calculated risks, brainstorm, and experiment, all of which are good for developing creative thinking abilities. Mentorship can help people who want to be CEOs get through the difficulties of a constantly changing business world. Leadership development through mentoring programs is an investment with a high return on investment (ROI), helping executives reach new heights and leave an indelible mark on the corporate world.

5. Confidence and Resilience Development

It's not easy to become a great CEO or business leader. You will face problems and setbacks along the way. Training from a mentor is an important part of building confidence and strength. When leaders are going through tough circumstances, they can lean on their mentors for encouragement and guidance. Their personal experiences, both successful and unsuccessful, teach us the importance of sticking with something even when things go sour. Aspiring leaders can get the confidence to take chances, face obstacles head-on, and conquer adversity with the help of a mentor who has faith in their abilities and provides constant encouragement.

Setting Yourself Up for Promotions

It could be difficult to find your way to promotion and positive recognition in a new workplace. Depending on the company's structure, there are several ways you can get noticed quickly and possibly be promoted. While establishing rapport with influential people plays a major role in more traditional hierarchies, collaboration and open dialogue may take precedence under flatter structures.

No matter the company's culture, it's important to carefully exhibit your leadership skills. Make sure you know what you're doing, build a strong personal brand, and look for ways to show leadership. You can speed up your career if you take the initiative to show what you can do. To assist you in reaching your professional objectives, I have put together the following list of tried-and-true methods.

Take a Look at Past Performances

- Have you ever been able to prove that you can get things done?

- Do you consistently contribute to the team's success?

- Is your credibility high?

- Have you rectified previous mistakes?

It's important to show that you've been successful in the past in this job. To achieve this, you must constantly show that you are a leader, produce high-quality work, and reach beyond your goals.

Strengthen Your Capacity to Lead Consistently

Taking leadership classes, taking on extra responsibilities, and challenging yourself are all great ways to hone your leadership abilities. Currently, I am focusing on forming informal book clubs to help people improve their skills. For 15-20 minutes, once a week, these groups get together on Zoom to talk about a book. Every month, they cover a new novel. By saving time and removing any social pressure to attend every week, this method creates an ideal setting for participants to constantly work on their skills.

Build Trustworthy Relationships

The key to success in any company is cultivating solid relationships with all of your coworkers, peers, and other stakeholders. Strive to be known as a leader who gets along with others and gets things done. Give a hand to those around you so they can achieve more success.

Sponsor Others through Networking

Even while networking is necessary for advancing one's profession, the majority of people do it for self-promotion. Well, you know what genuine leaders do? They advocate for other people. They don't miss a chance to connect people with one another, and they're always listening for ways they might be of greater service. Go to industry events, join groups for people in your field, and make an effort to help others if you're having trouble with this ability.

Express Yourself Clearly

If you want to advance in your career, you should let your manager know. Find out what else you can do to improve as a leader, and then do it. Simply mentioning your interest in a new position could help picture you in that role.

Take the Lead

Always be on the lookout for ways to get involved more, whether it's through formal or informal volunteer work inside your business. By proving that you are prepared to undertake bigger roles, you demonstrate that you are equipped to take on new responsibilities.

Developing Your Own Personal Brand: Molding Your Career Persona

To thrive in today's cutthroat business climate, personal branding—the process of intentionally molding how people see you—is essential. In the eyes of your supervisors, peers in the field, and coworkers, it acts as a compass, directing your behavior and relationships.

Find Your Voice

Finding your own special sauce, your own flavor, and the things that set you apart from the competition are the first steps in building your brand. Put your best foot forward by crafting an engaging personal statement that explains your value and showcases your skills and experience.

Establish Your Credibility: The Influence Online and Off

In this digital era, it is really important to establish a professional presence. Make sure your online identity matches your personal brand by building a strong presence on platforms like LinkedIn. Make sure that when you're offline, your interactions with other people always support the same story, so that you come out as unified.

Collaboration: Expanding Your Reach

When you work with others, you can increase your impact and exposure. Collaborate with coworkers on projects, show up to industry events, and help out with group efforts. You can add to your skill set and boost your personal brand by participating in these activities and being associated with successful collaborations.

Maintain Integrity

Building a strong personal brand is all about being genuine. Maintain integrity in all dealings, speak what you believe in, and be consistent in your messaging. Behaving consistently helps people trust you, which in turn strengthens your reputation and creates long-lasting relationships.

Time Management for Emerging Leaders in Business

A key differentiator for effective leaders in today's fast-paced corporate world is the ability to effectively manage their time. Time is of the essence as you climb the corporate ladder so you must be strategic and effective with how you use each moment. The key to efficient time management is not merely increasing output, but also coordinating daily activities with long-term objectives.

Walking the Road with Purpose

The map to successful time management is setting goals that are both clear and attainable. Make sure your short-term and long-term goals are in line with your career goals. With these objectives in mind, you may go about your day with confidence and focus. Your goals should be reviewed and adjusted on a regular basis to keep up with your changing priorities and professional path.

Paying Attention to What Really Matters

The key to efficient time management is setting priorities. Not every job is equally important, and it's very important to understand this. Sort your to-do list by importance and urgency so you may devote your time and effort where it will have the greatest influence in helping you achieve your objectives. Apply the 80/20 rule: Zero in on the small number of activities that have the biggest impact on your success and devote all of your energy to those. To stay on top of things and adjust to new situations, you need to regularly reevaluate your priorities.

Optimizing Your Day for Ideal Results

Future business leaders need to learn how to organize their schedules well in order to handle their time well. Depending on their importance and the amount of energy they require, set aside certain blocks of time for various tasks. Prioritize activities that demand your undivided attention and make sure your schedule matches when you are most productive. Incorporate breaks to avoid exhaustion and boost overall output. Stay flexible while staying committed to your long-term objectives by reviewing and adjusting your calendar on a regular basis to account for changing priorities and unexpected obstacles.

Organize Your Time Efficiently

Executives of the future must master the art of time management in this digital world. Discover a wide range of tools and apps that can improve your productivity, project management, and job automation. Software that helps you keep track of tasks, manage projects, and stay organized can make all the difference when it comes to meeting deadlines. Embrace technology that suits your needs and helps you work more efficiently. Make sure your time management tactics are up-to-date and flexible by regularly updating and refining your toolset to include new technology and methodologies.

Task Delegation

One of the most important skills to have as a company leader is the ability to delegate. Realize that you need help from others and that delegation is a smart way to empower your team. The key to a productive and cooperative workplace is assigning responsibilities that play to each team member's strong suits. To make sure the allocated responsibilities go smoothly, make sure everyone knows what to expect, provide them what they need, and set criteria for success. By dividing up tasks across team members, you not only lighten their load but also foster an environment where everyone works together to achieve common goals. If you want to be able to focus on the things that really matter and help achieve your leadership goals, you need to take stock of your duties on a regular basis and look for ways to delegate.

Cut Down on Distractions

Even the best-laid plans can go off the rails when something comes up. Should you want to be a successful business leader in the future, you need to be able to spot and deal with possible problems before they happen. Make sure you have a quiet place to work where you won't be interrupted. Try using time-blocking tactics, where you set aside particular blocks of time to work uninterrupted. Take advantage of technological solutions to temporarily disable Facebook, Twitter, and other not-so-important applications while you're working. Set boundaries with your coworkers and let them know when you need to concentrate on work. If you want to be a good leader, you need to make sure that your time is being spent wisely by regularly evaluating and adjusting your environment to find and remove disruptions.

Minimize Multitasking

Even while it may appear like a good way to save time, multitasking usually ends up making you less efficient and lowering the quality of your work. Leaders of the future must learn to zero attention on a single activity at a time. If you want to improve your efficiency and accuracy, focus on one thing at a time. Take a moment to center yourself before shifting gears to focus on a new task at hand. Mastering the art of multitasking will lead to better time management and higher-quality work.

Make Time for Rest

To be more productive, you need to take breaks, which goes against the idea that working nonstop makes you more productive. You can avoid burnout and keep your emotional and physical health in check by building planned breaks into your schedule. Incorporate brief periods of physical activity, stretching, or stepping away from your workstation into your workday. When you take longer breaks, like lunch, you may replenish your batteries, which in turn helps you be more creative and focused when you get back to work. Take time to relax and unwind so you can keep performing at your best as a leader.

Chapter 6:

Growing Within Your Organization

The growth and development of people is the highest calling of leadership.
—Harvey S. Firestone

If you want to be a great leader in your business, you have to go beyond managing people and instead motivate, guide, and drive structural change. Learn the ins and outs of "Growing Within Your Organization," and picture a leadership style that transcends the bounds of conventional management. It sums up the skill of leading large teams, controlling costs, and understanding multifaceted processes.

Leadership in organizations is complex, involving many different aspects. In it, leaders play an orchestral role, guiding the company's and its employees' development. This is more than just a management manual; it's a road map to being an agent of good change and a spark for advancement.

Discover the many facets of influence and learn how to make a bigger splash as a leader while also boosting your team's performance. When you begin this journey, imagine yourself as more than just a manager; imagine yourself as a powerful catalyst for change, influencing the future of your company. Once you finish this chapter, you will have the skills to lead your organization through its challenges and become a game-changer.

Getting Recognized as an Expert in the Field

Achieving long-term success and influence requires you to establish yourself as the trusted leader in the company you work for. Detailed below are some of the most important areas to consider when you consider strategic ways to establish yourself as an authoritative figure. Raise your profile to that of a reliable leader in your company.

- Without a defined purpose and specific objectives, it is impossible to lead. To what extent do your goods and services address customer pain points? To what extent are you planning to broaden your clientele? Your next step, after defining your company's purpose and objectives, should be to paint a picture of its future for your staff that will inspire them to care just as much about its success as you do.

- After you've planned out the future of your company, make sure that everyone on your team can understand it by communicating it effectively. Use many mediums to convey your ideas, including written word, visual aids, audio, video, and even one-on-one meetings.

- It is not about giving orders or giving advice when it comes to small company leadership and communication. The greatest leaders are interested in their people, sympathetic to their struggles, and encouraging of their ambitions; they are also excellent listeners and communicators.

- Honesty is a hallmark of good leadership. Their goal is to create trustworthy environments where employees feel comfortable enough to provide their honest opinions on what is and isn't functioning.

- Make no promises you can't keep, and your staff will do the same. Establish a climate where your team feels comfortable being forthright about their ability to complete tasks within the allotted time and resources.

- When you're your own boss, you presumably know how to handle everything that comes up with payroll. Show your staff that you're not asking too much by helping out around the office, whether it's making sales or mopping the floors. If you work side by side with them, your employees will be more motivated to work hard for you.

- It should be clear to your workers that you don't expect them to answer emails after business hours, work extra hours all the time, or come in sick. Leading a small firm effectively entails setting a good example of professionalism and maintaining attention during normal work hours.

Invest in Your Employees' Growth

The best leaders do more than just help their teams succeed in the here and now; they also plot a course for even greater success in the future. Knowing when people on your team are prepared to take on more responsibility or advance in their careers is important. To help them reach their full potential, mentors should prepare them for more responsible positions within and outside of the company. Create and maintain mentoring relationships outside of your organization to better equip your employees for career options. Keep yourself updated on industry news and trends, be an active member of your professional association, and push your colleagues to do the same. The return on investment (ROI) from mentorship programs continues for years to come as mentees go on to great things, whether as business partners or entrepreneurs.

Recognize When You Need Outside Help

Besides knowing what your workers' strengths and weaknesses are, you should also know what yours are. As your firm expands, you'll inevitably need to bring in experts to handle the more complex activities that you were formerly capable of doing alone, including billing. You can set a good example for your employees by admitting when you need help, showing them that you aren't perfect, and knowing when to seek an expert's opinion.

Patience Is Key in Times of Crisis

Great leaders are able to remain calm in the face of uncertainty. When the future is uncertain, they know that owning a small business entails navigating through unpredictable economic cycles. They can calmly adjust to both rapid expansion and more gradual plateaus.

When you are stuck, tell your employees that you don't know what to do and ask for their help. It will show that you appreciate their skills and suggestions. In the midst of a crisis, it is essential to relay the company's fundamental principles to the employees so that they can regain their composure and feel less threatened.

Making a Greater Impact

What is the best way to get people to follow you at work? The key to success is increasing your influence with your coworkers. Respect must accompany the action though. Gaining sway in the workplace has numerous advantages. Here are some pointers to help you or your team improve your ability to influence others in a professional and courteous manner.

Establish Trust and Bridge Gaps

One of the most important aspects of being a good leader is building trust. Always be there when your teammates need you, be dependable, and show them that you care. Make an effort to develop genuine relationships with coworkers beyond the scope of your professional encounters. Building genuine connections is at the heart of networking, which goes beyond simple card exchanging.

Keep an Open Mind and Value Opinions

Being a good listener shows respect and helps people understand one other. Welcome other points of view, promote honest discussion, and be open to new ideas. You may make everyone feel heard and valued by valuing differing viewpoints.

Stay Up to Date

Always be one step ahead of the curve when it comes to your career by making the most of opportunities to network, study trade journals, and attend conferences. To keep your leadership relevant and up-to-date with industry developments, you need to be nimble and quick to respond.

Prove Your Mastery

Stay current on all the latest happenings in your field, including best practices, emerging technology, and trends. When you show off your knowledge, people feel comfortable following you, and you even motivate them to do the same. Mentor coworkers, lead learning sessions, and add to the pool of communal knowledge; share what you know freely.

Keep Your Head Down and Admit When You're Wrong

Building trust and sincerity with your team is as simple as admitting when you're mistaken. Show perseverance and a development mentality by viewing setbacks as chances to learn. If you want to build trust and foster a culture of constant growth, be a modest leader.

Get to Know the Why Behind Your Coworkers' Moves

Acknowledge and comprehend that every team member is driven by their own specific goals. Adapt your leadership style to suit the needs of your followers, whether they are seeking approval, independence, or development opportunities. Team involvement and performance are both improved by this tailored approach.

Promoting Team Success

Leaders accomplish great things through effective teamwork. When employees learn to collaborate effectively, the whole company benefits. A lot of managers fail because they can't get their teams to work together. Companies can achieve unprecedented levels of financial success when their leaders master the art of cooperation. A leader's communication skills should be such that they inspire their team members to put the team's success ahead of their own. If you want your employees to work successfully together, follow these guidelines that effective leaders use:

Outline Who is Responsible for What

First and foremost, everyone on the team needs to know their specific job description. Avoid misunderstandings and maximize productivity by outlining the specific responsibilities of every team member. An atmosphere of unity and productivity can be created in the workplace when each individual knows how they contribute.

Use Individual Talents

Find out what each team member is good at and play to their strengths. To maximize output, work should be distributed in a way that plays to each worker's strengths. Promote team members' participation in cross-training programs to increase their skillsets and promote flexibility and adaptability.

Display the Virtue of Teamwork

Set a good example by working together with others. Show a sincere desire to work with others, communicate openly, and listen attentively. Inspire a sense of camaraderie among team members by creating an atmosphere that values collaboration above rivalry.

Take Part in Events That Foster Teamwork

Plan outings, workshops, or team-building activities that include a wide range of participants. Beyond just encouraging teamwork, these pursuits improve communication, forge stronger bonds, and provide the groundwork for trust. The ability to overcome obstacles and work together effectively is greatly enhanced in a well-connected team.

Encourage Responsibility

Make everyone on the team take responsibility for their actions and promises. To stay on track and complete projects on schedule, it's helpful to check in and provide updates on progress often. Inspiring people to take pride in what they do encourages them to do their best work.

Incentivize Outstanding Team Achievements

To strengthen a strong team culture, it is important to celebrate accomplishments as a group. Note important accomplishments, completed projects, and outstanding collaboration. Giving credit where credit is due is an effective way to boost morale and productivity on the team.

Being a Catalyst for Change Inside the Company

Changes in technology, shifting consumer preferences, and the emergence of new competitors all have an impact on internal dynamics in businesses. Since change is inevitable, a plan to deal with it is vital. Employees require outside inspiration, encouragement, and guidance to conquer their personal change resistance and propel the change initiative forward. Organizational change agents, outside consultants, or change leadership from within the company are all potential sources of this kind of assistance.

Create a Focused Vision

To kick off a change, an agent of transformation must first paint a clear picture of the ideal future condition. As a guiding light, this vision shows the way to achievement. Get the word out about this vision so everyone is pulling in the same direction. What matters most is not just making a change, but rather seeing a good transformation that inspires everyone.

Express Yourself Clearly

Good communication is the key to a successful transition. Expound on the "why" of the move, describe its advantages, and lay out the steps to take next. The key to fostering passion and trust among team members is to be approachable and transparent. The transformation journey can be better understood and embraced through communication, which is more than just exchanging facts.

Form an Alliance

It takes more than an individual's will to propel change; we need everyone's help. Important stakeholders and influencers should band together. These people do more than just provide their support; they actively promote the change. The weight of their endorsement encourages broad support and dedication.

Inspire Others

Giving people on your team the tools they need to become invested stakeholders is the key to a successful transformation. Give them responsibility, let them work on their own, and make them feel like they own something. In this way, you may create a setting where people are willing to participate in and take responsibility for the transformation. A strong and flexible team is built on empowerment.

Adapt to Change

Because of its very nature, change is difficult to foresee and frequently takes unexpected turns. The key to successfully navigate through times of uncertainty and difficulty is to be adaptive. Being adaptable lets you make changes and corrections when you need to. Being resilient in the face of ever-changing circumstances and welcoming the unexpected are key components.

Take On Resistance

Many people resist change because they are afraid of the unknown or because their routines are too deeply entrenched in the status quo. Keep an eye out for this pushback, figure out where it's coming from, and deal with concerns with empathy. When dealing with resistance, it's important to understand people's concerns, reassure them, and create a supportive environment so they can handle the change.

Track Development

To successfully navigate change projects, it is crucial to continuously analyze the progress being made. The best way to keep tabs on progress is to use metrics, invite feedback, and set milestones. By regularly assessing progress, we can make sure we're on track to meet our objectives and make any necessary adjustments to stay the course of change.

Get Over Your Failures

Problems are opportunities for learning, not impediments. As agents of change, we should see setbacks not as failures but as chances to grow and improve. Strategic modifications can be made to strengthen resilience and empower the team with knowledge to overcome future obstacles by understanding the fundamental causes of setbacks.

Strive for Excellence

There is no such thing as a one-time event that brings about change. Inspire the employees to always strive for betterment. Motivate them to think creatively, learn new things, and be flexible. To succeed in a dynamic and ever-changing environment, organizations must cultivate a culture of continuous improvement, where change is seen as an evolutionary force.

Striving for Optimal Performance

Improving processes, goods, or people via regular analysis of performance, discovery of possibilities, and implementation of small but significant improvements is known as "continuous improvement." It's all about cutting down on waste, pushing up quality, and driving efficiency. Leaders who practice continuous improvement are better able to adapt to the ever-shifting dynamics of the market. It necessitates an attitude of continuous improvement, openness to new ideas, and learning. A few important points are these:

Models and Frameworks

- **Kanban**: Seeing the work, controlling the flow, and encouraging small changes over time.

- **Lean:** Getting rid of waste and finding the best way to give value.

- **Scrum:** Uses iterative rounds, retrospectives, and flexible planning.

Useful Tools and Techniques

- **Gemba Walks:** A way to watch how work is done where it happens.

- **Kaizen Events:** Short classes that focus on making things better.

- **Root Cause Analysis:** Figuring out what the real problems are.

The role of leadership is to encourage continuous improvement, provide tools, and encourage people to have a learning mindset.

Personal Growth at Work

Fostering a strong workplace culture relies on personal growth, which is more than simply an individual effort. Learning new things, improving existing ones, and achieving worthwhile objectives are all part of this ever-changing process. If we want to build a workplace that values happiness, productivity, and health, we must acknowledge its importance for leaders and team members alike. What follows is a more in-depth examination of the ways in which professional development affects office dynamics:

Approach to Continuous Improvement

Actively seeking out learning opportunities, attending workshops, and acquiring new skills should be a priority for leaders, as they are the driving force inside a business. Adopting a growth mindset not only motivates team members to do their best, but it also guarantees that leaders can keep up with the dynamic and ever-changing nature of their careers. Companies can help this happen by giving their employees access to appropriate learning materials, full training programs, and mentorship opportunities.

Backing from Employers

When it comes to encouraging team members to develop personally, leadership is key. Leaders may do more than just set an example; they can also offer practical assistance in the form of tuition reimbursement, career counseling to help employees figure out what they want to do with their lives, and formal leadership development programs. This kind of backing not only shows that you care about your team members' development as people, but it also fosters an environment where you can really shine in your career. The workplace is transformed into an environment that recognizes, supports, and celebrates the growth journey of every individual.

Interactive Element

Let's look at the **Force Field Analysis,** which is a useful way to understand and handle change in a business. Let this interactive activity be your guide as you go through each phase of the process.

How Does Force Field Analysis Work?

Examining the elements or forces impacting an intended result is the goal of Force Field Analysis, a method for managing change and making decisions. You may use it to find the factors that are pushing for change as well as the ones that are holding it back. You can develop a strategy to make the most of beneficial influences and lessen negative ones while implementing change by examining these forces.

To do a force field analysis, follow these steps:

1. **Define the Change:** Clearly explain the change or improvement that you want to make. On your analysis sheet, write it in the middle of a box.

2. **Brainstorm Driving Forces:** Make a list of all the things that are pushing for the change. These can be issues inside or outside the company.

3. **Brainstorm Restraining Forces:** Think of the things that are stopping the change and write them down.

4. **Weigh and Score Each Factor:** Rate each force on a scale from 1 to 5 that shows how strong or weak it is. Combine the scores for the forces that are pushing and pulling.

5. **Picture the Analysis:** Make a picture of a force field. Arrows can be used to show how strong each force is compared to the others. The force is bigger when the arrow is longer.

6. **Assess and Execute Your Action Plan:** Pick out the things that can be changed or influenced. Make a plan to make moving forces stronger and

stopping forces weaker. Consider ways to make moving forces score higher or restraining forces score lower.

You can better understand the possibilities and threats of change with the help of Force Field Analysis. You may make smart choices and draft efficient change management strategies by using this approach. Embrace change inside your workplace with this helpful tool.

Chapter 7:

The Well-Being of a Leader

Self-care is not selfish. You cannot serve from an empty vessel. —Eleanor Brown

It is easy to lose sight of the basic truth in Eleanor Brown's astute words in the never-ending quest for leadership greatness. It is easy to put our own needs last when we are leaders because of the immense pressure to meet everyone else's expectations. But a leader's perseverance, along with their strategic ability, is what makes a good leader. This chapter delves into the deep link between a leader's health and their ability to lead effectively throughout time.

A leader's mental, emotional, and physical health all interact with one another in complex ways. As we delve into the complex world of self-care, you'll find that putting yourself first isn't a selfish thing to do, but rather a strategic necessity. The objective is crystal clear: To provide you with self-care skills that are crucial for managing the complex difficulties of leadership and leaving a lasting, fulfilling legacy.

Going beyond the usual stories, we take a more comprehensive look at leadership here. Get ready to learn how a leader's health directly affects their ability to motivate followers, think creatively, and maintain a dynamic leadership style. This chapter will serve as a guide for you to follow if you want to be a leader who is not only effective but also one who stands the test of time.

The Signs of Stress in the Workplace

The health of workers and the efficiency of businesses are both negatively affected by stress in the workplace. It happens when a person's ability to handle work obligations is inadequate. There are several potential causes of stress in the workplace including, but not limited to, disagreements, frequent changes, and threats to job security.

Health and safety officials at the federal level have linked stress in the workplace to extended absences from work (Better Health Channel, 2012). It is important to note that stressful experiences are subjective because people's perceptions of them differ depending on the type of work they do, their personality traits, and other personal characteristics.

Stress in the workplace can take many forms, impacting people's emotional and physical health. As leaders, we must be able to spot these warning signals in our own team members and in others. These are the main signs:

1. Stress-Related Body Symptoms

- Always being tired or worn out, even after getting enough rest.

- Digestive problems like gut discomfort, gas, or indigestion are called "gastrointestinal upsets."

- Stress-related anxiety causes headaches or migraines that happen often.

2. Signs of Psychological Problems

- Less work getting done, mistakes, missing deadlines, or not being able to concentrate.

- Changes in mood that can't be explained, such as a shift from anger to sadness.

- Getting angry or short-tempered easily with coworkers or tasks.

3. Indicators of Behavior

- The tendency to withdraw from social engagements, shun team members, or experience a disconnection.

- Decreased involvement due to a lack of interest in or passion for one's work.

Why People Get Stressed Out at Work

Workplace stress is a complex issue that can arise from many different aspects of a worker's job. It has far-reaching consequences for businesses and their workers. Even when the economy is doing well, job uncertainty is always a possibility because of things like layoffs, mergers, and bankruptcies, which cause big changes for workers. In the aftermath, there are often more tasks, higher demands for output, less benefits, and lower salaries, which all contribute to a stressful work environment. Many different types of workplace stress have been identified, representing the wide range of difficulties that people encounter in their varied occupations.

Fear of Losing Employment

Anxieties and stress levels among workers are already high due to the constant worry of possible layoffs. A person's mental and emotional health are affected by the strain of not knowing how long their employment will last. Contractual instability, which is common in temporary or project-based jobs, adds fuel to the fire of job insecurity. There is a general decrease in the mental resilience of the workforce due to this disturbing environment, which impacts both individual performance and the state of mind.

Harassment

Whether it's subtle bullying or overt prejudice, mental health suffers when people endure mistreatment. These kinds of events have a domino effect on a person's mental health, impacting their stress levels and general well-being. These problems are made even worse by a toxic work environment where employees are treated poorly by their supervisors and coworkers. These difficulties must be addressed if we want to create a workplace where people feel appreciated and supported, creating an environment that helps people be mentally and emotionally resilient.

Not Having Enough Resources

Lack of tools and equipment creates big problems that make it hard for workers to do their jobs well. Not only does a lack of necessary resources reduce production, but it also causes stress. It gets worse when you don't have enough support, whether it's from upper management or your coworkers. Employee happiness and productivity are both negatively impacted in a workplace that does not provide enough support systems. If we want to create a healthy workplace and improve the health of our employees as a whole, we must address these resource-related issues.

Unhappy Workplace Relationships

Managing relationships at work can have a major effect on my health and happiness. Stress levels rise when there is conflict and tense relationships, which are marked by problems that are not resolved or arguments that do not go away. Dealing with such difficulties can be emotionally draining and impede career advancement. When relationships with coworkers or superiors are strained, it can lead to a loss of social support, which in turn can cause feelings of loneliness. Employees can better handle the stresses of the job and reach their full potential when they are able to form strong bonds with their coworkers.

Leadership Approach

The dominant leadership style of upper management greatly influences the culture of the company. Tension and a lack of open communication are symptoms of authoritarian leadership, which is marked by strict, top-down methods. This management style creates an environment where employees could feel restricted and overwhelmed. Another big cause of stress at work is bosses who don't care about their employees, which shows when they ignore their problems or needs. The development of a leadership style that encourages transparency, empathy, and quick action can be vital for creating a positive and encouraging work environment, which in turn improves the health of employees.

Stress-Reduction

It is our paramount duty as leaders to create a welcoming workplace for all employees. If you want to accomplish this with your team, you should think about using these stress-reduction tactics:

Organizational Strategies:

- Make sure that both the job and its expectations are defined clearly.

- Get everyone on the same page by clarifying their individual responsibilities.

- Evaluate each person's abilities and assign responsibilities appropriately.

- Workloads should be matched to resources so that workers aren't overworked.

- Establish peaceful, well-balanced work areas.

- Improve the lighting, air flow, and look of the whole area.

Personal Approaches

- Motivate your staff to make self-care a top priority.

- One way to build resistance to stress is to make sure you get enough sleep, eat a balanced diet, and exercise regularly.

- Make sure your employees learn how to be assertive so they can deal with problems better on the job.

- Encourage employees to communicate their wants, needs, and limits.

- Engaging in regular physical activity has a calming effect on the body and mind.

- Incorporate stretching, yoga, or short walks within your workday.

- Make sure your staff knows they can talk to you about anything.

- Handle matters with compassion and speed.

Integrating Work and Life: A Comprehensive Strategy

Beyond the conventional idea of work-life balance, there is a way of thinking called work-life integration. It stresses the importance of integrating professional and personal lives so that they supplement and support one another rather than separate them. Let me tell you what's important:

The goal of work-life integration is to have work and personal life flow together naturally. People need to understand that their personal and work lives are connected. Where work-life balance sets strict limits, work-life integration lets you be flexible and change. Rather than focusing on rigid time boundaries, integration professionals strive to optimize their overall well-being.

Why Work-Life Integration Is Beneficial

- With work-life integration, you won't have to separate your professional and personal lives in your mind. By seeing everything as interconnected, people are able to put aside their differences and work together harmoniously.

- The goal of integration is not equal distribution but rather the promotion of a complementary perspective on work and life.

- Professionals can now prioritize their calendar adjustments with the help of integration. It could involve staying late at the office to finish a personal project or checking personal emails while on the clock.

- Instead of strict time constraints, the emphasis is on efficiency and satisfaction.

- Work-life integration acknowledges that happiness isn't just about being productive at work. It includes spending time with loved ones, taking care of one's health, engaging in recreation, and unwinding.

- Make time for fun and pleasure in life.

Tips for Balancing Work and Personal Life

The first step in striking a healthy work-life balance is making a realistic timetable for yourself. Get more done in less time by setting priorities according to how important each activity is and how much energy you have. The trick is to not take on too much at once and to fight the urge to overschedule yourself. For long-term efficiency and less burnout, this is the way to go.

Set up a routine for working from home: It's important for people who work from home to have a regular habit. Work, breaks, and individual duties should all find a happy medium in this schedule. Avoid burnout and strike a good work-life balance by setting clear limits and working certain hours. Remote workers benefit greatly from routines because they give them the framework they need to manage their work and personal life well.

One important aspect of fostering work-life integration is highlighting the need for flexibility. Encourage employees to take charge of their own time management by giving them the freedom to create a timetable that works for them. Occasionally being flexible, like going to a family event while on the clock, shows that you value your personal obligations. Flexibility fosters a more favorable and tolerant work environment while also helping employees maintain a healthy work-life balance.

Another useful tactic for achieving a healthy work-life balance is cross-training individuals to do different types of work. This activity adds variation to their regular tasks while also improving their skill set. Employees with a wide range of abilities are better able to balance their work and personal lives, which in turn allows them to be more versatile and adaptable in their work and personal life management.

It is really important to teach managers how to spot when their teams are under stress or unbalanced. Providing managers with the tools they need to communicate effectively allows them to have honest conversations about work-life balance with their employees. Managers who have received this training will be better able to listen to their employees' issues and offer the assistance they need to build a culture that prioritizes the health, happiness, and work-life balance of all employees.

Mindfulness

To be a mindful leader is to engage in daily self-reflection and interpersonal relationships with an attitude of compassion, openness, and complete presence. A mindful leader is one who makes developing their own insight, competence, and self-control a top priority. Doing so enables them to gracefully handle high-pressure circumstances, which in turn motivates their team members to surpass expectations.

Both mindfulness and empathy are at the core of a thoughtful leader's leadership philosophy. Leaders that invest time in getting to know their teams, listening to their issues, and adjusting their approach to leadership in response foster an atmosphere conducive to development on all fronts.

Reflection

A person's understandings, emotions, and experiences can be better understood through reflective thinking, which is an ongoing process. It happens either during or after an activity and gives us a chance to learn a lot from the results, both good and bad.

A powerful tool for transformation, reflection enables leaders to assess their plans with a critical eye. The best leaders are able to find the insights that fuel continual growth by analyzing past successes and failures. Along the way to becoming a better leader, it can serve as a benchmark for evaluating methods and encouraging a growth mindset.

Advantages of Reflection and Mindfulness for Leaders

- Leaders who practice mindfulness are better able to avoid dwelling on the past or worrying about the future.

- By taking stock of their actions and thinking about what may have been different, leaders can improve their decision-making in the future.

- Leaders who are mindful listen, understand, and connect with their team members.

- When we take the time to reflect, we may better comprehend ourselves and the world around us, which in turn improves our communication skills.

- Leaders who practice mindfulness are better able to deal with stress and failures because it strengthens their emotional resilience.

- Strong leaders are able to reflect on their experiences, grow from them, and adapt to new circumstances.

- Leaders can evaluate their methods with objectivity when they practice mindfulness and reflect.

- Leaders have the ability to assess how well their strategies are working and make necessary adjustments.

Consistent mindfulness practices are great for leadership development. Meditation, deep breathing, and attentive awareness are all practices that leaders can include in their day-to-day lives. Also, they need to make reflection a regular part of their schedule so that they may think critically about their behaviors, choices, and relationships.

Terry Borten's "What, So What, Now What?" Model of Reflection

There is a methodical way to reflect using the Terry Borten Model. A leader's approach is to begin by outlining the "What" of the scenario or event, and then to assess the "So What" by thinking about the good and bad parts. Last but not least, they use the new knowledge to chart a course for future improvement by deciding what to do next ("Now What") (Ochoa, 2023).

Basic Skills for Mindful Leadership

Focus: Being able to keep your attention on a problem while fixing it is one of the most important skills in mindful leadership. Leaders that practice mindfulness are better able to focus their teams' attention when it wanders, which in turn helps people understand difficult situations and make good decisions.

Clarity: Mindful leaders are great at seeing things as they really are, without making assumptions that can affect their judgment. Their ability to see things as they really are helps them face obstacles head-on and makes it possible for them to make well-informed decisions.

Innovation: Mindful leaders must practice openness of mind in order to improve the cognitive processes that result in innovative ideas. They motivate their teams to think creatively and solve problems by creating an atmosphere of inquiry and openness.

Compassion: Leaders who practice mindfulness make decisions while keeping in mind the interconnectedness of all people. They are able to lead with empathy and foster a welcoming workplace for all employees because of this essential talent.

The Role of a Healthy Body in Good Leadership

We leaders tend to put a premium on managing teams, making tough decisions, and plotting long-term strategies. Having good physical health is essential, but it is easy to forget about it. Being healthy has far-reaching effects on a leader's capacity to do their job well. Let's take a look at why leaders should prioritize their health, how exercise helps with stress, and some practical ways to get moving regularly.

Less Stress and Better Mental Health: Exercising has a direct effect on lowering stress levels. Our bodies release endorphins, which are natural mood boosters when we exercise. These feel-good endorphins are great for relieving stress and making you feel good overall. Exercising regularly also gives a good way to release bad feelings. For leaders to stay focused and make good judgments, stress management is essential.

Better Decision Making: Physical activity has a positive effect on brain function. It trains our brains to function more efficiently and calmly under duress. To make sound decisions when pressured or confronted with difficult situations, a healthy brain is necessary. Exercising helps improve one's decision-making and problem-solving skills.

Physical Relaxation: Deep breathing, yoga, and other stretches can help you relax physically. Loss of muscular tension helps alleviate stress in the body all throughout. Leaders who make time for physical fitness tend to deal with stress better and are better able to keep their cool under pressure.

How Physical Exercise Shapes Self-Control and An Eye for Success

Regular exercise does more than only make you fit; it also helps you develop the self-control and focus on your objectives that are essential for good leadership. Sticking to a fitness program teaches people self-control, which helps them in many other areas of life. Those in leadership positions who make exercise a priority are more likely to excel in multitasking, prioritizing, and maintaining focus.

In addition to developing tenacity and resilience, exercise instills a goal-oriented mindset. Achieving fitness goals, such as completing a certain distance run or lifting a certain weight, teaches the value of setting and working towards attainable, long-term targets. This kind of thinking allows leaders to accomplish corporate goals through efficient project management, well-thought-out strategies, and other means. When it comes to being a leader, the things you learn in the gym are very useful.

Making Little Changes Every Day Can Have a Big Effect

A leader's health can benefit in the long run from establishing daily habits that emphasize physical exercise. Consistency is key, so make exercise a regular part of your life by setting attainable objectives and finding creative ways to move around, even if it's only walking the stairs or stretching during breaks. Over time, these routines have an effect on more than just physical health; they also affect psychological and emotional wellness. When leaders make exercise a regular part of their lives, it shows that they care about being healthy and gives them the energy to keep going.

Prioritize Self-Care: Building Leadership Resilience

Leaders must prioritize self-care, which includes maintaining good sleep hygiene and managing stress. Emotional and cognitive resilience are both strengthened by making quality sleep a top priority. Being mindful, meditating, or practicing relaxation methods can help leaders deal with stress in a healthy way. Leaders can better face adversity and make wise choices when they take care of themselves emotionally and mentally. Leadership resilience is built upon the practice of self-care.

Lead by Example: Promoting Health by Personal Dedication

By setting a good example, leaders can greatly contribute to encouraging well-being. Taking part in business wellness initiatives, writing about personal fitness experiences, and generally showing that you care about your physical health are all ways to lead by example. A leader's ability to set an example and encourage others to do the same is a key component of effective leadership. Leaders may help create a health-conscious work environment by setting an example of good lifestyle choices themselves.

Showcasing Vulnerability

Leadership that shows they are human and talks about their health and happiness freely fosters a more compassionate and understanding workplace. It is important for leaders to be open and honest about their own health struggles and when they need time to recharge. By opening up about their own struggles, leaders humanize the wellness discussion and make it more accessible to everyone on the team. Incorporating this strategy into the workplace creates an environment where employees feel heard and valued while they try to improve their overall health.

The Importance of Cultivating Emotional Intelligence for Successful Leadership

To be a good leader, you need emotional intelligence (EI). Beyond logical reasoning and technical know-how, it impacts leaders' capacity to recognize, comprehend, and control their own and others' emotions. As leaders, we need to be able to identify our own emotions, talents, shortcomings, and what sets us off. We have to be self-aware enough to know that our feelings influence our actions and choices. Leaders that are self-aware are able to control their emotions and make deliberate decisions.

Good leaders are able to rein in their emotions, keep their cool under pressure, and adjust to new circumstances. They are able to keep their cool and not react emotionally when things get tough. Resilience and flexibility are fostered through self-management.

A leader who is socially aware is empathetic. They have excellent social awareness, are able to read group dynamics, and value other points of view. Strong relationships are fostered by leaders who are socially conscious and who promote inclusive settings.

A Leader's Emotional Intelligence and Its Effects

Organizations can equip leaders with EI training to help them become more self-aware, empathetic, and adept at developing relationships. Emotional intelligence, stress management, and communication skills are the main areas covered in training programs.

Rather than remaining constant, emotional intelligence develops through time and experience. Leaders should always be pushing themselves to learn more and improve their emotional intelligence. Courses, coaching programs, and workshops offered online all help with continuous improvement.

How Developing Emotional Intelligence Can Benefit You

- EI improves flexibility, collaboration, and decision-making.

- Leaders with high emotional intelligence encourage innovation and calculated risks.

- Attracting and retaining talent is much easier in an upbeat work atmosphere.

- EI increases productivity and contentment in the workplace.

- Acquiring EI paves the way for promotions and leadership positions.

Chapter 8:

The Well-Being of a Leader: Specific Techniques for Stress Management

It's not the load that breaks you down, it's the way you carry it. —Lou Holtz

It is our duty as leaders to make judgments, satisfy expectations, and juggle a multitude of tasks. Our health and our capacity to lead are both threatened by the crushing burden that these responsibilities might take on if we aren't careful. Part 2 of our wellness exploration takes us on a path toward specialized methods for dealing with stress, that sneaky enemy that can bring down the strongest leaders.

You will find a wealth of useful information and techniques for dealing with stress in this chapter, which acts as a guide. We know that stress isn't just an annoyance; it's a major hindrance to good leadership. You will have a customized stress-management toolbox—a set of practical tools to help you handle the leadership responsibilities with poise, equilibrium, and resilience—by the end of this chapter.

Building a Toolbox for Resilience

The capacity to recover quickly from failure, adjust to new circumstances, and keep your composure under pressure is a hallmark of strong leaders. Leadership is a constant balancing act between the needs of the business, the dynamics of the team, and our own development as individuals. When these responsibilities start to pile up, it can be detrimental to our health and productivity.

Emotional Resilience

Your energy levels are directly related to how you're feeling emotionally. Do what you can to recharge yourself because fatigue can make your feelings worse. Developing regular routines—like going for a walk first thing in the morning, meditating, or spending time with loved ones—helps build emotional resilience. Learn to say "No" when you need to in order to keep your emotional energy levels up and set firm boundaries to avoid emotional burnout.

Recognize that feelings are normal reactions. If you're having trouble coping with strong emotions, try writing, deep breathing, or grounding activities. You can view problems as chances for personal progress by using positive reframing, a powerful practice. Get help from someone you trust, such as friends, mentors, or counselors, when you feel like your emotions are getting the best of you. Feeling better and getting new perspective are two benefits of talking openly about how you're feeling.

If you want to learn to be more present and less stressed, try mindfulness meditation. Practicing mindfulness can greatly improve one's emotional regulation and general health. As you consciously tense and release muscle groups, you will experience a gradual release of tension, which is known as progressive muscle relaxation. Art, music, and writing are all forms of creative expression that can help people deal with difficult emotions and find peace in their lives. Adopting these habits helps strengthen your emotional resilience, which in turn makes it easier for you to handle the challenges of leadership without losing your composure.

Physical Resilience

Get plenty of sleep. Both your mental and physical health depend on getting enough sleep. Aim for seven to nine hours of high-quality sleep nightly. Establish a regular bedtime routine, turn down the lights, and minimize screen usage in the hours leading up to bedtime.

Make exercise a part of your everyday routine. A good mood, less stress, and more resilience are all benefits of regular exercise. Pick anything you love doing, whether that's yoga, dancing, or running. Physical and mental health can be improved through movement.

Eat a wide range of plant-based foods, along with nutritious grains, lean meats, and healthy fats. A healthy diet helps the body bounce back from challenges. Remember to drink enough water—not enough water can lower your energy and brain function.

Mental Resilience

By making meditation a regular part of your life, you may train your mind to be more self-aware and less judgmental. This technique has multiple benefits, including improving focus, reducing anxiety, and increasing cognitive flexibility. Simple practices like mindful breathing can help you stay in the here and now, which in turn can strengthen your mind and make you more resilient.

Embrace challenges with open arms since they are chances to grow and learn. With a growth mentality, you can see failures not as fatal blows but as opportunities for personal development. Instead of getting stuck in self-pity, take a step back and objectively analyze what went wrong. From this, draw what lessons you can and figure out how to apply them going forward. Switching perspectives like this makes people more mentally tough when things go rough.

A lifelong dedication to curiosity will nourish your brain's resiliency. Keep your mind active, seek out new information, and explore uncharted territory. Reading widely, even outside of your area of expertise, broadens your horizons and encourages mental agility and flexibility.

Social Resilience

Nurture deep relationships with those you work with, as well as those you're close to at home. Resistance to stress is enhanced by social support. Engaging in attentive listening while interacting helps to cultivate understanding and empathy. Saying "Thank you," and "I appreciate it," helps bring people closer together.

It's okay to be vulnerable and seek support when you need it. If you want to improve, ask reliable people for their thoughts. Become a member of a peer group or professional network. Gaining support and new insights from connecting with people who share similar interests is a great feeling.

Meditation and Mindfulness

Stress and burnout are real consequences of constantly pushing yourself to perform at a high level, meet strict deadlines, and produce tangible results. Methods of relaxation and mindfulness can be useful in such situations. These techniques can help company leaders be more effective, less stressed, and create a healthier work atmosphere.

Do brief sessions first. Take a few moments to sit in silence and concentrate on your breathing. Take note of your breathing without judgment as you inhale and exhale. Mindful breathing, even for only a short while, can help alleviate stress.

Incorporate mindful breathing into your daily routine. Take a moment to focus on your breathing while you wait for a meeting, commute, or just enjoy a break. You can use it to calm your nerves and clear your head.

As a form of meditation known as "mindfulness," the focus here is on the present moment and how you are feeling without judgment or analysis. Just sit quietly, breathe deeply, and gradually bring your attention back to the breath when you feel your mind wandering. Transform your life with the power of mindfulness meditation.

Relax in a comfortable position, whether lying down or sitting upright. Gently direct your awareness to various areas of your body, taking note of any feelings without attaching any judgment. The practice of body scan meditation can help alleviate stress and anxiety by bringing awareness to specific areas of the body.

How to be a Mindful Leader

A good leader knows how to set acceptable boundaries and when to say "No." You can avoid burnout, protect your personal time, and keep your work-life balance by setting boundaries. Take these tactics into account:

Set Boundaries

Think about what's important to you and what you stand for. Do you have any priorities? Set clear limits on your personal time, work hours, and email contact.

Get Good at Saying "No"

Realize that declining an offer does not indicate a lack of strength. You can safeguard your health in this way. When asked to do more than you can handle, politely say "No."

Make Good Use of Delegation

Rely on your staff and give them responsibility. Allow other people to take charge so that you may clear your head.

Taking Time Off to Relax

A lot of the time, business leaders are under a lot of pressure. Intentional stress breaks are highly important for staying focused and avoiding burnout:

- Stop for short periods of time throughout the day. Take a break from your workstation, stretch, and focus on your breathing. Take these little moments to refuel.

- Get out into nature. Being in nature helps to relax the mind. Get out of your head and into nature for a while; you'll feel better thereafter.

- Occasionally, step away from electronic devices. Put your phone on silent, don't check email, and give your brain a break.

Having a Career Coach Help You

If a leader is looking to improve their overall performance, overcome obstacles, and establish meaningful goals, a career coach can be an invaluable resource. These coaches not only provide leaders with insightful feedback but also hold them accountable and devise individualized plans for development. Companies benefit greatly when their executives work with career coaches to help them clarify their goals, hone their leadership abilities, and reach their maximum potential.

Ways for Leaders to Manage Their Time and Set Priorities

Business leaders frequently face the challenge of managing several duties, deadlines, and competing expectations in an ever-changing environment. Their emotional and physical health may suffer as a result of the constant demands placed on them to perform, make important decisions, and provide outcomes. If they want to be stress-free, productive, and have a good work-life balance, company executives must learn to manage their time and priorities effectively.

Cutting Out Needless Tasks

Time-wasting behaviors can decrease productivity; therefore, it's vital to detect them and handle them. Performing audits of time allocation on a regular basis is one successful method. For leaders, the key to streamlining is identifying repetitive activities that don't provide value. Another way to avoid interruptions and keep focused work periods intact is to set specific times each day to check email and social media. It is important for leaders to use their judgment when accepting meeting invitations; if the agenda is unclear or doesn't mesh with overall goals, dismiss the invitation. By using a strategic approach, time is invested with purpose, leading to optimal efficiency and the development of meaningful leadership.

Getting Over Procrastination

Targeted methods can help leaders overcome the frequent obstacle of procrastination and be more effective. As part of the "Eat the Frog First" strategy, you should tackle the hardest thing first thing in the morning. This will give you a feeling of accomplishment and get you started on the right foot. To avoid feeling overwhelmed, break down major projects into smaller, more manageable steps. Then, celebrate each milestone as you reach it. One effective strategy to combat procrastination is to set self-imposed deadlines. Through the use of these strategies, leaders foster a proactive attitude, guaranteeing that tasks are addressed effectively and laying the groundwork for ongoing productivity.

Streamlining Meeting Processes

Leadership success hinges on productive meetings. A well-defined agenda helps keep meetings on track, gets people thinking forward, and makes the most efficient use of everyone's time. Meetings that are time-boxed with fixed durations encourage participants to be on time and to the point. One way to make sure everyone is holding themselves accountable and keeping tabs on their progress is to summarize the session's action items and obligations at the end.

Efficiently Devoting Time to Every Task

Effective time management involves setting aside specific blocks of time to work on individual tasks, rather than trying to juggle too many at once. To better keep tabs on due dates, milestones, and dependencies, try using a project management application like Asana or Trello. Project check-ins at regular intervals enable prompt adjustments and the removal of possible obstacles.

How to Delegate Work Efficiently

Delegating not only reduces workload reduced, but also empowers team members and fosters growth. It also ensures that the right individuals handle the correct duties. That said, delegation isn't always easy to implement. Managers may be hesitant for a variety of reasons including insecurity, a lack of confidence, or the conviction that they are capable of doing a better job on their own. Refusing to delegate, on the other hand, can cause fatigue, stunt team growth, and reduce productivity in general.

Leaders need to be able to delegate duties effectively, and knowing what to delegate is critical. It is possible to delegate many of the day-to-day tasks to others; however, some tasks do require close supervision from upper management. Leaders should put their energy into areas where they can make the biggest impact and let others take care of the things that aren't their strong suits. Assigning projects that encourage team members to grow and develop is also vital.

A successful leader knows the need to strike a balance between micromanaging and delegating. When you delegate too much, you run the risk of burnout; when you delegate too little, your skill goes unused. Open dialogue, frequent feedback, and progress updates are key to finding this middle ground. Leaders should provide direction without imprisoning innovation, fostering a setting where team members are encouraged and enabled to thrive.

The interests, skills, and strengths of each team member should be taken into account by leaders while delegating duties. At its best, teamwork is achieved by giving tasks to individuals who are particularly good at certain things. When delegating tasks, it's important to meet regularly to review progress and offer direction. By focusing on the big picture and rewarding originality, leaders may inspire their teams to achieve better results.

Avoiding confusion and making sure everyone knows their part requires clear directions. A great way to boost morale is to openly recognize and celebrate team members' achievements. Leaders should not suffer from Superman Syndrome; instead, they should delegate tasks, build trust, and give their team members the authority they need to succeed.

Chapter 9:

Decisive Leadership and Problem-Solving

Problems are only opportunities in work clothes. —Henry J. Kaiser

In the world of leadership, where opportunities and threats are always present, the insightful words of Henry J. Kaiser serve as a map, leading us through the complexities of making quick decisions and addressing problems. This chapter takes you on a journey into the core of leadership, where challenges become opportunities for individuals skilled at navigating the intricate decision-making process.

To strengthen the bedrock of leadership, the next pages provide an in-depth examination of the complexities of decision-making and problem-solving. Learn to avoid typical mistakes, encourage creative problem-solving among your team members, and come out stronger than before. This chapter goes beyond just talking about leadership; it takes readers on an immersive journey that will equip them with insights and practical wisdom.

Mastering the Art of Good Leadership Decision-Making

At its foundation, effective leadership is based on sound decision-making. Decisions that affect our teams, companies, and stakeholders are always present to us as leaders. Every decision we make has an impact, whether it's about distributing resources, tackling difficult challenges, or determining future strategies. Let's take a look at the fundamentals that enable leaders to make smart, meaningful decisions.

Rational Thinking

Logic is a cornerstone of leadership, necessitating analytical thought and critical examination. Complex problems can be navigated by leaders who are good at breaking them down, seeing patterns, and making logical conclusions. They can use this talent to their advantage by dissecting complex issues into their component parts. When making judgments, leaders must be able to critically evaluate information, identify their own biases, and look at things from several perspectives.

Solving Problems

Expert problem-solving, including investigating causes at their source and considering alternative solutions, is at the heart of good leadership. In order to find solutions, problem-solving leaders use techniques like the 5 Whys analysis and the fishbone diagram to get to the bottom of things. The best ideas come from those who are encouraged to think outside the box and who participate in regular brainstorming sessions.

Psychological Competence

Leadership that makes a difference requires emotional intelligence, which includes qualities like self-awareness and empathy. When making judgments, leaders who are in tune with their emotions take into account the impact those decisions will have. With emotional intelligence, they are able to control their emotions, keep their cool, and not make hasty decisions. One of the most important qualities a leader may have is empathy, which helps them understand how their decisions will affect their team and other stakeholders.

Decision Kinds

When you're a leader, you have to make choices of different types, such as operational, tactical, strategic, and policy choices. Strategic decisions influence the course of an organization over the long term, whereas operational decisions deal with the day-to-day duties. While policy decisions lay out broad principles, tactical decisions connect these domains.

Divergent thinking is essential for effective leadership, since it promotes the development of several options through teamwork. Leaders can benefit from decision trees, which are visual tools that assist them map out choices, probabilities, and probable outcomes. When decision-makers use strategic visualization and divergent thinking, they improve the decision-making process.

Making smart decisions involves weighing the pros and cons carefully. Careful risk management is a leadership competency; leaders weigh the benefits and drawbacks of each option. Decisions with significant consequences revolve on the equilibrium of risk and reward. To round out their examination of possible repercussions, leaders employ cost-benefit analysis, which compares and contrasts advantages and disadvantages taking into account monetary, social, and environmental factors.

Building a Culture of Problem-Solving on a Team

The ability to solve problems is more than just a skill in today's fast-paced business world; it's an attitude that promotes creativity, adaptability, and expansion. When faced with obstacles, opportunities, and problems, a team's ability to solve them and reach its goals depends on its culture of problem-solving. Let's explore the key elements of cultivating this kind of culture by utilizing knowledge from different sources.

Acknowledge the Issue

A paradigm shift is necessary to initiate a problem-solving culture that views issues as opportunities for progress rather than roadblocks. Recognizing that an issue exists and that it develops when expectations differ from reality is the first step. Teams should be honest about their problems and work to resolve them openly rather than hiding or downplaying them. It's important to keep problems detached from people, not to place blame, and to see them as learning experiences. Organizations can facilitate productive problem-solving by cultivating a culture where recognizing problems is promoted, rather than feared.

Establish a Safe Environment

When it comes to handling problems effectively, creating a psychologically safe space is important. Establishing a safe space for team members to thrive in is a critical leadership responsibility. The safety net is secured by an environment that promotes fearless expression, allowing employees to freely express their problems, make observations, and provide solutions without worrying about being judged.

Get to the Bottom of It

In order to solve a problem thoroughly, it is necessary to investigate its origins. Successful leaders use systems thinking to see the big picture, not just the symptoms, and to comprehend how everything is interrelated.

Ideation Session

When people work together to generate ideas for solutions to problems, innovation takes flight. Lots of ideas come from welcoming other points of view and encouraging people to look beyond the box. Since quantity is important, teams come up with a plethora of ideas before evaluating them. When people from different departments work together, it increases creativity because it brings new perspectives and ideas from all around the table.

Implement and Oversee Solutions

It is just as important to successfully execute a solution as it is to solve the problem itself. In order to effectively execute their goals, leaders must create detailed plans, delegate tasks, establish due dates, and allocate resources. Checking up on progress and seeing how solutions are playing out in the real world requires regular feedback loops. Constant efficacy and progress are guaranteed by this flexibility.

Leaders need to exhibit deliberate serenity when faced with uncertainty. Better decisions are the result of pausing to consider all of one's options and then settling on the best one. Maintaining composure helps leaders on an individual level, but it also sets an example for the whole team, encouraging them to be resilient and solve problems effectively.

Stay Away from These Typical Leadership Pitfalls

Here are some potential problems and ways to avoid them:

- Put off making a big decision until you have all the facts; then, seek advice from professionals. Don't make snap decisions.

- The skill to adapt is important, even if you think that prior experience is enough. Stay updated and adapt constantly.

- Too much time is given to people who don't do well to improve: Quickly resolve any concerns with performance. Establish precise goals.

- Focus Loss: Set strategy goals as a top priority. Avoid getting caught up in details.

- Avoid Being Too Self-Concerned: Being a leader is all about putting other people first. Keep in touch with the greater goal.

- Failing to Adopt a Fresh Perspective: Leaders need to change. Welcome change and adjust to new circumstances.

Mastering Office Politics

Professionals at all levels of an organization's hierarchy need to be adept at navigating office politics. How you proceed in your job is greatly affected by how you understand how offices work. Take a look at every strategy for navigating politics effectively:

One of the most effective ways to succeed in politics is to be yourself. To establish trust, be honest and forthright. Build relationships that last by acting in accordance with your principles and not by acting in a role or pretending.

When interacting with people in a politically charged setting, it's best to assume the best of their intentions. Strike a balance between defensiveness and curiosity; instead of reacting defensively, try to grasp rationale.

Consider *"How can I make a contribution?"* instead of *"What can I gain?"* and adopt a service mindset. By focusing on helping others, you can have a positive impact, earn people's favor, and grow a support system of people who believe in your abilities.

Make connections. The point of networking is to make connections that matter. Get out of your office, take part in projects, and talk to people who aren't on your team. Make time for relationships on a regular basis to ensure their support in the long run.

Identify powerful people in the company. Find those people who hold significant sway within the company. Get to know them, ask for their counsel, and benefit from their wisdom. Having a good rapport with influential people might help you gain access and perspective.

Set things right with your boss. Make it a habit to meet with your boss on a regular basis to review progress, ask for advice, and make sure everyone is pulling in the same direction. Building a solid relationship with your line manager is essential for successfully managing office politics.

Get over your work stress to end rivalries. It's best to deal with issues head-on, look for areas of agreement, and concentrate on common goals. Show your competitors that you value them and are open to working with them if it means you can both succeed.

Use your expertise. Make strategic use of what you know and can do. Be an authority in your field, contribute your knowledge to build credibility, and take part in conversations to the fullest.

Cultivate lasting connections. Developing lasting connections takes time and effort. Pay attention to coworkers outside of work, congratulate them when they succeed, and be there for them when they're going through terrible times.

Learn your company. Get a feel for the ins and outs of your company's norms, policies, and chains of command. Learn how people make decisions so you can adjust your tactics appropriately. To successfully navigate corporate politics while preserving integrity and furthering your career, you must have a firm grasp of the subject.

Part 3:

Evolving, Adapting, and Excelling in

Leadership

Chapter 10:

Staying Adaptable in a Changing Business World

It is not the strongest of the species that survive, nor the most intelligent, but the one most responsive to change." —Charles Darwin

When we look into what it means to be flexible in the business world, which is always changing, this deep understanding will help us stay on track. In this chapter, you will learn the tricks of being flexible in a dynamic corporate world. In this series of pages, we will try to give you a bird's-eye view of why adaptability is so important in today's fast-paced corporate world, and not just as a talent.

With the information and tools we provide, you will be able to not only survive but thrive in an environment where change is never-ending. As we delve into the significance of looking forward to trends and embracing continuous learning, you'll find out how adaptability may change your life.

Recognizing Career Growth Dynamics

Like living ecosystems, our careers are in a perpetual state of change, shaped by both internal and external forces. The experiences, decisions, and goals that make up your professional path are unique to you, whether you're a recent college grad entering the field or a seasoned CEO thinking about retiring.

Stagnant vs Dynamic Careers

To have a dynamic career, you need to be able to seize opportunities, adjust to change, and measure your progress. People that have successful jobs are open to trying new things, have a growth mindset, and are always looking for ways to improve themselves. Taking on new responsibilities, moving up the corporate ladder, and embracing professional shifts are all examples of careers that are always evolving.

A stagnant career, on the other hand, doesn't grow or move forward; people stay in the same role without learning new skills. Reluctance to change, a lack of drive, and a failure to acquire new skills are all signs of a profession that isn't moving forward. Being in the same job for a long time without moving up the ladder or taking advantage of chances to learn and grow are both examples of professional stagnation.

Personality Traits and Skills

The cornerstones of professional success are skills, both hard and soft. "Hard skills" refer to concrete competencies like programming or language fluency, while "soft skills" refer to more subjective qualities like communication and collaboration. Skills are important since they help build a complete professional profile, which is something that companies look for.

Personal traits, in addition to your skill set, are an important part of any thorough professional profile. Trust is vital in the workplace, and integrity—which includes honesty and reliability—builds it.

Market Trends and Socio-Economic Considerations

By looking into the complicated web of socioeconomic dynamics, we can see the many factors that influence career routes. The paths that people take in their careers are heavily influenced by factors like socioeconomic status, level of education, societal expectations, health, gender, and various government initiatives. Experts in social economics analyze these factors to understand how they affect economic activity, which can help you make informed career decisions.

In today's fast-paced business world, it's important to stay on top of changes in industries, technologies, and the global economy. Being able to adjust to these constantly changing market trends is important for staying relevant in your job and getting ahead. To successfully navigate the ever-changing professional landscape and make strategic decisions, this knowledge is vital.

Professional Growth and Strategy

Careful strategic planning is required when charting a course for professional advancement. To achieve success, it is necessary to align short-term aims with larger, more far-reaching ambitions. Make sure your career advancement is both strategically beneficial and personally satisfying by conducting an in-depth assessment of your interests and degree of job happiness.

Embracing Change: A Guide to the Unknown

We must be able to welcome change and uncertainty since our world is dynamic, unpredictable, and ever-changing. Success in handling any kind of transition—

whether it's a personal one, an organizational one, or a global disruption—is heavily dependent on our thinking and the techniques we employ.

The Way Uncertainty Works

Life is full of uncertainties. It affects both our private and public lives, testing our capacity to change and persevere. The COVID-19 pandemic, along with changes in the economy, new technologies, and geopolitical tensions, has made us more cognizant of the fact that we cannot predict the future. We should not be afraid of uncertainty, but rather see it as a chance to develop, expand, and create.

The Ability to Adjust to New Situations

We rely on our ability to adapt in times of uncertainty. It entails:

- Being able to shift gears and alter direction when necessary is the essence of flexibility.

- Learning Agility: The ability to pick up new information and abilities quickly.

- Quickness: Adapting quickly to changing conditions.

A Change in Thinking Framework

To deal with unpredictability, you need to start a mental paradigm shift. Start by letting yourself feel uncomfortable as you shift from a rigid "know-it-all" mentality to a more adaptable "learn-it-all" one. Recognize that thoughts and emotions are fleeting and engage in self-reflection to activate your internal consciousness, which is like turning on a dormant gadget, so you may more consciously comprehend reality, relationships, and life's lessons.

Developing a Growth Mentality

Promote a growth mindset by challenging yourself to get better every day. A more adaptive and relevant outlook on failure would be to embrace lifelong learning. Don't say, *"I can't do it."* Instead say, *"I can't do it yet,"* acknowledging that setbacks are necessary for progress in both your personal and professional lives.

Pay Attention to What's Important:

Amidst a flood of information, learn to zero in on what really matters. Become better at ignoring unimportant details, blocking off distractions, and focusing on what really matters. Present-moment awareness makes thoughtful interaction with surroundings, emotions, and experiences possible, while self-reflection helps assess objectives, values, and progress.

Looking Ahead to Potential Trends

Organizational effectiveness depends on anticipating and adapting to changing business trends. It is our responsibility as leaders to anticipate future changes rather than react to them.

No More Legacy Thinking

If a company wants to evolve, its leaders must break free from legacy thinking. Embrace disruptive methods, encourage a culture that values innovation and risk-taking, and question long-held beliefs. To be ready for future problems, companies need to be innovative and agile, which can only be achieved by challenging norms and trying new approaches.

Welcome to the Digital Age!

For success, digitization is a must. Simplifying processes, unlocking important data, and enhancing client experiences are all made possible by digital tools. Successfully utilizing technology guarantees agility, quick response to changes in the market, and a competitive advantage in this age of digital transformation.

Using Analytics Software for Predictions

Data can be mined for insights and future consequences can be foreseen with the help of predictive analytics. To stay ahead of the competition, firms must be able to spot patterns, optimize their strategy, and proactively reduce risks. Decisions in many areas of the company might be based on data, both historical and real-time.

Executing a Trend Study

A well-executed trend analysis will have clear objectives, sufficient data, appropriate statistical methods, and the ability to analyze results in order to draw useful conclusions. To address changes in consumer behavior, market conditions, or operational demands, it is helpful to understand trends across time.

Keeping an Eye on Major Trends

Pay close attention to megatrends, which are societal and industry-wide movements at the macro level. Changes in demographics and technical developments are two examples of disruptive factors that must be understood. Businesses can weather social and economic storms better if their strategies are in sync with megatrends.

Anticipating Environmental Uncertainty

Uncertainties in the environment test the resilience of businesses. Evaluate potential dangers, plan for how to deal with them, and incorporate eco-friendly procedures. In order to ensure long-term sustainability, it is necessary to assess potential risks associated with climate change, resource constraint, and new regulations.

Adapting to Current Trends in Business Strategy

Business strategy must be adjusted in response to ever-changing market conditions. Organizations may adapt to different futures, improve their collaboration, and connect their corporate objectives with social impact by using purpose-driven strategies, ecosystem thinking, and scenario planning. Being nimble allows you to adapt to changing market conditions.

Leadership and Continuous Learning

To thrive in today's fast-paced corporate world, leaders must be willing to learn new things on the job. Leaders need to be flexible, able to adjust to new situations, and encourage creative thinking. Leaders that commit to lifelong learning are better equipped to anticipate and adapt to changes in their fields, build a wide skill set, and solve problems more effectively. Furthermore, it helps foster a growth mindset in companies by encouraging participation from workers and constructing a setting that encourages exploration, new ideas, and the exchange of information.

A leader's ability to adapt their knowledge, abilities, and perspectives to a dynamic and unpredictable reality depends on his or her commitment to lifelong learning. This dedication to continuous learning not only boosts efficiency in the workplace, but also helps one reach their full potential as an individual. A leader who is committed to lifelong learning not only demonstrates this value to their colleagues, but also develops the flexibility and fortitude to adapt to a dynamic and unpredictable environment.

Chapter 11:

The 20-Minute Daily Leadership Routine

The key to success is to focus our conscious mind on things we desire, not things we fear.
—Brian Tracy

Leadership is an ever-changing field, where success is achieved via deliberate and consistent behavior. In this last chapter, you will learn about "The 20-Minute Daily Leadership Routine," a powerful yet simple formula for developing your leadership abilities and bringing your thoughts into harmony with your goals.

This chapter serves as both a conclusion and an implementation of the knowledge gained from the previous chapters. It requires action as well as reading. All it takes to become an exceptional leader is 20 minutes a day to cultivate qualities like self-awareness, resilience, good communication, and adaptability.

The Significance of a Daily Routine

By providing a consistent framework for everyday activities, routines can offer structure, boost productivity, and reduce stress. A regular schedule makes it easier to form good habits, get a handle on one's time, and make steady progress towards one's long-term objectives. In addition to helping with focus, efficiency, and creating discipline, routines are great for managing competing priorities. Because of its beneficial effects on mental health and the flexibility it provides, it helps people persevere when faced with adversity. A daily routine can be a powerful tool for self-improvement and career advancement by providing structure, direction, and mastery over environment.

Goals and Advantages

1. Pay Attention to Improving Important Elements of Leadership:

Minutes 0–5: Elevating Your Communication Abilities

Set aside some time in these first few minutes to go over a communication principle. Participatory listening, offering helpful criticism, or any other applicable principle could fall under this category. Put this theory into action in a simulated or real-life situation, like creating an email or participating in a role-playing game. Take some time to think about what you did and write down any things you could change after the exercise.

Minutes 5–10: Emotional Intelligence Enhancement

Effortlessly transition into pursuits that boost emotional intelligence. Try a reflection or mindfulness practice to get in touch with your feelings and learn how they influence your behavior. To work on your empathy, try putting yourself in the other person's shoes and thinking about a recent conversation. Take careful notes during this activity if an emotional management technique comes to mind.

Minutes 10–15: Enhancing Decision-Making Abilities

To move on to developing better decision-making abilities, think back on a decision you made recently and the steps you took to reach that conclusion. Make note of any prejudices that may have played a role in your choice and suggest a way you could improve your decision-making skills. This may necessitate expanding your data analysis, consulting with more people, or rethinking your decision-making process.

Minutes 15–20: Improving Teamwork and Problem-Solving Skills

At the end of the session, focus on ways to improve your collaboration and problem-solving abilities. Jot down your thoughts about a recent team discussion or problem-solving experience. Choose one thing that worked and one that might be better. Make a mental note of what you can do in your next team engagement— whether it's suggesting a more organized way to solve problems or encouraging more honest dialogue—to improve collaboration and problem-solving skills.

2. Ensuring You Stay On Track With Your Goals

Example 1: Standard (Daily)–20 Minutes at a Time

Incorporate this model procedure into your regular leadership practice. By covering essential aspects of leadership in a reasonable amount of time, it offers a well-rounded strategy. You can tailor it to your needs and make it bigger as you progress in your leadership journey.

3. The Process and How It's Done:

Option One: Complete Each Step Faster

Once you've mastered the fundamentals, you can always move on to more challenging routines, but the basic ones will get you started. But Option One, which involves spending less time on each piece without sacrificing thoroughness, is what this chapter is about.

Adaptability and Personalization

Flexibility is the key to the beauty of the fundamental routine. It is a starting point from which you can tailor it to your specific situation, goals, and requirements. You may discover that it helps to modify the routine more as you advance in your leadership path. Here are some suggestions for adapting the standard procedure to meet changing needs or personal tastes:

Changing the Distribution of Time:

Reduce the length of each component to make room for other important tasks if time is of the essence. Dedicate fewer minutes to each portion while keeping the fundamental framework, making sure the program is reasonable and maintainable.

Adding New Components

You may want to add certain things to your regimen if your leadership goals change. In order to hone your leadership skills even further, you may need to complete certain assignments, study certain books, or participate in other activities. Find a way to keep yourself challenged without letting your everyday schedule suffer as a result.

Adding More Time to the Regular Schedule

Increasing the time of the routine is a good choice for people who want a more involved daily leadership experience. The overall time might be extended to 30 minutes or more, allowing for a more thorough examination of each leadership feature, or new components could be introduced to the routine.

A Deeper Dive into the Routine

Sample Routine: Advanced

Duration: 20 minutes

Frequency: Daily

Minutes 0–3: Building a Solid Base of Knowledge

To get in the swing of things, go back to a fundamental leadership concept or the most important thing you learned from a recent resource. Think about how this new information enhances your leadership style in general.

Minutes 3–6: Concentration and Mindfulness

If you're having trouble focusing, managing stress, or just want to start your day off on the right foot, try practicing mindfulness. A centered mentality is essential for effective leadership, and this core exercise creates just that.

Minutes 6–9: Development and Improvement of Leadership Abilities

Get down to the serious business of developing your leadership abilities. Focus on developing specific abilities, such as active listening, providing constructive criticism, or digesting input from others, within a broader domain like effective communication. To evaluate your development, take a quick look back.

Minutes 9–12: A Point of Connection for Developing Relationships

Pause for a second and focus on the people in your business network. Little things, like taking the time to write a note or give a coworker, mentor, or teammate a quick call, add up to a helpful and cooperative workplace.

Minutes 12–15: Leadership Development, Adaptation, and Success

Think back on a difficult situation you were in recently and how you overcame it. Figure out what you can do with the knowledge you get to be more flexible in the future. Learning from experiences and striving for constant improvement are themes that run throughout this section.

Minute 15 to 17: Snippet for Continuous Learning

Make time in your schedule to read a short article or watch a quick video that will expand your leadership skills. This will help you continuously learn. Use this excerpt as a guide to keep up with the latest leadership news and trends.

Minutes 17–19: Review and Adjustment of Goals

Take stock of your leadership goals, rejoice in your successes, and revise them as necessary. As you react to new situations or comments, this step will keep your daily routine in line with your leadership goals.

Minutes 19–20: Making Moving Forward Plans

Find the most important thing to do today to finish the routine. Make sure it supports your leadership objectives and encourages you to do your best every day. Now that you've completed this last phase, you're prepared to lead outstandingly once again.

Customizing the Routine to Meet Your Specific Leadership Needs

Take this chapter's suggested daily routine as a starting point for your own leadership journey; it's a framework that can be bent and shaped to fit your needs. Consistency and intentionality are the keys, whether you go with the basic program, the advanced version, or adapt parts to fit your changing goals.

Leadership Case Study: Putting the Routine into Practice

In order to demonstrate how the routine is put into practice, let's take a look at a made-up scenario involving Sarah, a mid-level manager with leadership aspirations. Using it as a foundation, Sarah adjusts it to her everyday schedule.

Sarah's Daily Leadership Routine (Basic):

Minutes 0–5: Enhancing Verbal and Nonverbal Communication

Sarah goes over a communication principle again, this time with an emphasis on giving useful criticism. Through a role-playing exercise with a colleague, she puts this theory into practice in a simulated setting. She thinks about the interaction and makes a list of things she could change afterward.

Minutes 5–10: Developing Emotional Regulation Skills

Sarah focuses on the here and now by practicing mindfulness. In order to develop more empathy, she considers a recent difficult team conversation through the eyes of her teammates. When Sarah has to keep her emotions in check, especially during important conversations, she writes them down.

Minutes 10–15: Enhancing the Ability to Make Sound Decisions

In order to determine whether her recent decision was impacted by any biases, Sarah examines the decision-making process. Realizing the value of a balanced viewpoint, she lays up a plan to include more people's opinions in future decisions.

Minutes 15–20: Improving Teamwork and Solving Problems

While thinking back on a recent group effort, Sarah finds both the good and the bad. She makes a mental note to do something to help the team communicate better on the next project, with an emphasis on teamwork and free-flowing ideas.

Updates to Sarah's Daily Schedule

Enhanced Emphasis on Communication Skills:

Sarah chose to increase the allotted time for the communication section from four to six minutes after realizing how important it is to her work. Because of this change, she is now able to study communication theory and practice more thoroughly.

Exploring Decision-making in Depth:

Sarah, who is very dedicated to developing her capacity for sound decision-making, has resolved to examine her procedure for making decisions more thoroughly twice weekly. This necessitates setting aside a bit more time on those particular days to guarantee a comprehensive study. Sarah makes sure her daily practice fits in perfectly with her leadership path by making it fit her personal requirements and goals.

The End

Before wrapping up, leaders at all levels of their careers can benefit from the 20-minute daily leadership plan that is described in this chapter. Whatever version you choose—the basic one, the one with customization choices, or the more complicated one—the most important thing is to approach each minute with purpose. You may improve your present abilities and set yourself up for future growth and success as a leader by consistently applying these ideas. Leadership is an ongoing process, and this routine will serve as your daily map to help you reach your full leadership potential.

Conclusion

After reading the book, we've finally reached a turning point that will change our lives. The A.C.E. Leadership Progression Framework has served as our reliable map, allowing us to navigate the complex landscape of leadership development with precision, efficiency, and speed. It is fitting that, as we near the end of this illuminating journey, we take stock of the guiding concepts that have informed our view of leadership and how we practice it.

A: Awareness

A strong sense of self-awareness is essential for successful leadership. In this book, we have explored the depths of self-reflection, urging leaders to do the same. Recognizing that awareness is not an endpoint but an ongoing journey requires a steadfast dedication to self-awareness. The cornerstone of genuine leadership that connects with stakeholders and teams is self-awareness, which includes knowing one's triggers, limitations, and strengths.

C: Connection

At its core, leadership is all about people. Establishing trust, encouraging empathy, and providing emotional support are all pillars of the A.C.E. model. The capacity to establish genuine, personal connections with people is fundamental to good leadership communication. We have covered the many ways in which genuine relationships are the engine that drives an organization to success through the stories, activities, and examples offered here.

E: Execution

Without action, a dream is just a dream. Putting dreams into action is the most important part of the A.C.E. structure, according to the last pillar. By providing leaders with practical strategies and insightful information, we have helped them overcome the challenges of execution and turn their vision into a reality. Leadership theory is translated into impactful results through execution, which includes goal planning and decision-making.

As we say "Goodbye" to these pages, keep in mind that leadership is an ever-changing field. The A.C.E. Leadership Progression Framework can be adjusted to fit the dynamic nature of leadership and company, rather than being a strict formula. Changes in the environment necessitate adjustments to how we lead.

By condensing the core principles of executive coaching into 20 minutes each day, this book strived to provide a realistic and efficient path to becoming an expert leader. Engaging in regular self-reflection, creating connections, and putting strategies into action is not a chore but an investment with huge dividends.

Leadership is not an endpoint, but rather an ongoing process of development and improvement. As you continue your leadership journey, the knowledge and wisdom you receive from this book will be by your side. May you discover a new sense of self-assurance, strength, and proficiency as a leader as you incorporate the A.C.E. principles into your everyday life.

Finally, may this be the beginning, not the end. Now that you have the A.C.E. Leadership Progression Framework at your disposal, you can lead with conviction, enthusiasm, and purpose. Climb the corporate ladder of success, become an expert communicator, and welcome the life-altering influence of leadership advancement. The path ahead is open to you, and the opportunities are limitless.

If you found this book to be a valuable source, don't forget to drop in a review!

About the Author

Victor Greyson, a distinguished figure in executive coaching and leadership development, brings a wealth of experience and wisdom to the field at the age of 52. Renowned as the author of *The Executive Coaching Bible*, Victor seamlessly merges decades of corporate expertise with an innate talent for establishing connections, mentoring, and inspiring others.

With over three decades of practical expertise in the business world, Victor has guided the careers of many individuals, from eager new managers to seasoned C-suite executives. His latest publication stands as a testament to his proficiency, providing a concise and actionable guide designed to seamlessly fit into the hectic lives of today's professionals. Using in-depth case studies and innovative techniques, *The Executive Coaching Bible* equips its readers with everything they need to succeed at the highest levels of any organization with genuineness, focus, and self-assurance.

In addition to his professional achievements, Victor maintains a steadfast commitment to family, having shared 27 years of marriage with his wife and raised two accomplished children. He understands the connection between personal fulfillment, career advancement, and overall happiness, and he credits his family with giving him a strong foundation from which to launch his successful career. Beyond the transformative pages of his guide and the confines of corporate boardrooms, Victor's passion extends to global travels. He travels the world in search of cultural insights to incorporate into his one-of-a-kind teaching methods and books.

Glossary

1. **Leadership Skills:** Abilities enabling individuals to guide, influence, and inspire others, encompassing effective communication, decision-making, and emotional intelligence.

2. **Emotional Intelligence:** The capacity to recognize, understand, and manage one's own emotions and navigate and influence the emotions of others for improved interpersonal relationships.

3. **Decision-making Skills:** The ability to make sound and effective decisions by considering various factors, assessing risks, and weighing available options.

4. **Teamwork:** Collaborative efforts of individuals working together to achieve a common objective, involving effective communication, mutual support, and leveraging each team member's strengths.

5. **Problem-solving:** The process of analyzing, identifying, and resolving challenges or obstacles within a team or organization.

6. **Adaptability:** The capacity to adjust to new conditions, changes, or challenges, allowing leaders to navigate uncertainties and lead teams through evolving situations.

7. **Continuous Learning:** A commitment to ongoing personal and professional development through the acquisition of new knowledge and skills.

8. **Mindfulness:** The practice of being fully present and aware of the current moment without judgment, valuable for reducing stress, enhancing focus, and promoting well-being.

9. **Goal Setting:** The process of establishing specific, measurable, achievable, relevant, and time-bound (SMART) objectives to guide individual or team efforts.

10. **Routine:** A structured and consistent set of activities or habits designed to enhance productivity, well-being, and goal attainment.

References

Better Health Channel. (2012, January 6). *Work-related stress*. Better Health Channel. https://www.betterhealth.vic.gov.au/health/healthyliving/work-related-stress

Boksic, B. (2023, March 22). *Mindset The New Psychology of Sucess Summary, Review, Notes -*. Growthabit.com. https://growthabit.com/psychology-books/mindset-the-new-psychology-of-sucess-summary-review-notes/#:~:text=The%20purpose%20of%20Dweck

BrainyQuote. (n.d.). *Lou Holtz Quotes*. BrainyQuote. https://www.brainyquote.com/quotes/lou_holtz_120090

Brower, C., & Dvorak, N. (2019, October 11). *Why Employees Are Fed Up With Feedback*. Gallup.com; Gallup. https://www.gallup.com/workplace/267251/why-employees-fed-feedback.aspx

Businessolver. (n.d.). *STATE OF EMPATHY 018*. https://info.businessolver.com/hubfs/empathy-2018/businessolver-empathy-executive-summary.pdf

Cherry, K. (2023, February 22). *What Are the 9 Types of Nonverbal Communication?* Verywell Mind. https://www.verywellmind.com/types-of-nonverbal-communication-2795397#toc-why-nonverbal-communication-is-important

Crestcom. (2020, May 13). *6 Conflict Resolution Barriers You Need to Overcome*. Crestcom International. https://crestcom.com/blog/2020/05/13/6-conflict-resolution-barriers-2/

Dilmaghani, M. (2020). Beauty perks: Physical appearance, earnings, and fringe benefits. *Economics & Human Biology, 38,* 100889. https://doi.org/10.1016/j.ehb.2020.100889

Dragne, L. (2017, May 31). *The Basics of Nonverbal Communication (Part One)*. Great People Inside. https://greatpeopleinside.com/nonverbal-communication-part1/#:~:text=Peter%20F.

Goodreads. (n.d.). *A quote by Brian Tracy*. Www.goodreads.com. Retrieved November 30, 2023, from https://www.goodreads.com/quotes/881048-the-key-to-success-is-to-focus-our-conscious-mind

Grammarly Business. (2023, February 21). *2023 State of Business Communication report*. Go.grammarly.com. https://go.grammarly.com/business-communication-report

Horoszowski, M. (2020, January 21). *How to Build a Great Relationship with a Mentor*. Harvard Business Review. https://hbr.org/2020/01/how-to-build-a-great-relationship-with-a-mentor

Kohlrieser, G. (2022, August 19). *Resilient leadership: Easy steps to navigate the working life pressure*. Www.imd.org. https://www.imd.org/research-knowledge/leadership/articles/resilient-leadership-navigating-the-pressures-of-modern-working-life/

MAYHEW , J. (2021, March 24). *Storytelling for Leaders: What Makes a Great Story?* Virtualspeech.com. https://virtualspeech.com/blog/storytelling-for-leaders

McKenzie, C. L., & Qazi, C. J. (1983). Communication barriers in the workplace. *Business Horizons, 26*(2), 70–72. https://doi.org/10.1016/0007-6813(83)90088-5

Ochoa, D. (2023, July 28). *What So What Now What (Reflective Model & Examples)*. Thinkific. https://www.thinkific.com/blog/what-so-what-now-what/#:~:text=The%20What%20So%20What%20Now%20What%20model%20is%20an%20incredibly

Page, S. (2022, January 13). *57 Quotes on Wellness and Health to Inspire Healthy Living*. Info.totalwellnesshealth.com. https://info.totalwellnesshealth.com/blog/quotes-on-wellness-and-health

The CEO Publication. (2023, August 3). *Never underestimate the power of Communicating effectively at your organization*. Www.linkedin.com. https://www.linkedin.com/pulse/never-underestimate-power-communicating-effectively/

Webinopoly. (n.d.). *The Psychology of Color in E-commerce: How Color Choices Impact Consumer Behavior*. Webinopoly. Retrieved November 30, 2023, from https://webinopoly.com/blogs/news/the-psychology-of-color-in-e-commerce-how-color-choices-impact-consumer-behavior

Wei, J. (2015, December 30). *It Is Not The Strongest of the Species That Survive - Charles Darwin*. Due. https://due.com/not-strongest-species-survive-charles-darwin/